Richard Baxter

Full and Easie Satisfaction which is the True and Safe Religion

Richard Baxter

Full and Easie Satisfaction which is the True and Safe Religion

ISBN/EAN: 9783337296629

Printed in Europe, USA, Canada, Australia, Japan

Cover: Foto ©Lupo / pixelio.de

More available books at **www.hansebooks.com**

SATISFACTION WHICH IS THE TRUE AND SAFE RELIGION.

In a CONFERENCE

Between { D. A DOUBTER,
P. A PAPIST, and
R. A REFORMED CATHOLICK CHRISTIAN.

In *Four Parts:*

I. The true stating of our Difference, and opening what each Religion is.
II. The true case and full Justification of the Reformed or Protestant Religion.
III. The Protestants Reasons and Charges against Popery, enumerated.
IV. The first Charge, *viz.* Against Transubstantiation made good: In which Popery is proved to be the SHAME OF HUMANE NATURE, notoriously contrary to SENSE, REASON, SCRIPTURE and TRADITION, or the Judgement of the Antient and the Present Church; devised by Satan to expose Christianity to the Scorn of Infidels.

By *Richard Baxter.*

London, Printed, for *Nev. Simmons*, at the *Princes Arms* in St. *Pauls* Church-yard. 1674.

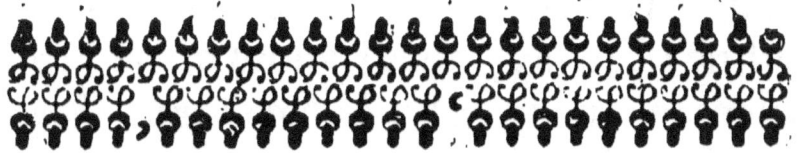

To his Grace the Duke of Lauderdail *His Majesties Commissioner, and Principal Secretary for the Kingdom of* Scotland, *&c.*

May it please Your Grace,

HOnour and Gratitude are affections much inclined to speak out, and to publish themselves in the predication of their objects: And seeing the Literate Tribe have long used so much boldness with Great Names, as to prefix them by Dedications to their Writings, I take that advantage to tell the world how greatly Your favour hath long since obliged me, and ſtill continueth ſo to do. And while I can ſay, that I know of no Nobleman living who *hath read more of my Writings* than You have done, all that know the *End of Writing*, will conſent, that there is no Noble Name which I ſhould prefer. And as I long ago read in the Learned *Spanhemius*'s Dedication of his *Dubia Evangelica p.* 3. to *You* (well joyned with the famous *Uſher*) the predication of Your *Judicium ſupra ætatem maturum, rerum omnium cognitione ſubactum pectus*, and that as atteſted by the *Illuſtrious Duke* of *Rohane*, the *Moſt Sagacious Arbiter of ingenies*; And years and experience have been long adding to Your knowledge: Being not a ſtranger to the Truth of this my ſelf, I have great reaſon to be Ambitious to *ſtand right in Your eſteem*: (For who reverenceth the Judgement of ignorant Readers?

Since I overgrew that Religion which is taken up *most* on *humane trust*, by increasing knowledge I increased mens displeasure; and my judgement not falling just into the mold of *any Sect* among *Church-dividers*, there is scarce *any Sect* which doth not, according to their *various interests*, signifie their displeasure. Some only by *Magisterial Censures*; *more credibly* acquainting the world, what they *are themselves*, than *what I am*, or what *is my judgement*. But from *others* I take a *meer slander* for *Clemency*, and as *Philostratus* saith, *de Dicto Phavorini*) *Et dum Socratis cicutam non bibam, æreâ privari statuâ non lædit. Simple Christianity* is *my Religion*: I determine to *know nothing* but *Christ Crucified* (and *Glorified.*) And I am past all doubt, that till *simple Christianity* become the terms of *Church-Unity and Concord*, the *Church will never see Unity or Concord*, which shall prove *universal* or *durable*. So certain am I, that the Wits of the *Learned*, much less

 of

of the *Community of vulgar* Christians, will never arrive at the stature, of *Concord*, *in numerous and difficult points*: Nor the *marvellous diversity* of *Educations, occasions, temperatures* and *capacities*, be *ever united* in any thing but what is *plain* and *simple*. And as Certain am I, that the *Universal Conscience* of *true believers* will *never unite*, in any thing which is not *evidently divine*. And yet as certain am I, that the forsaking of the determination of the *Holy Ghost* and the *Apostles*, Acts 15. 28. and of *Paul's Decision*, Rom. 14. & 15. hath been the *Engine* of *Church-Divisions* and *many calamitous distractions* to this day: And that that *blessed Prince* who must have the honour and comfort of *beginning* the *true healing* and *Concord* of the Churches, must pare off *all their superfluities*, and leave them at best among their *things indifferent*, and unite them on the terms of *simple Christianity*.

And as to *Popery* I have certainly found,

found, that the Crofs *Interefts* and *Pafsions* of Difputers have made us (though really too diftant) to feem commonly about *many Doctrinals more diftant* than indeed we are: And that it had been better with us, if fuch men as judicious *Ludov. le Blank*, had had the ftating of our Controverfies at the firft, that *differing words* and *methods* might not have paffed with either fide for *damnable errors* in the faith. I mean in the points of *fore-knowledge*, *predeftination*, *providence*, *predetermination*, *concurfe*, *original fin*, *free-will*, *univerfal Redemption*, *fufficient Grace*, *effectual Grace*, the *nature of Faith*, *Juftification*, *Sanctification*, *Merit*, *Good Works*, *Certainty of Juftification*, and of *Salvation*, *Perfeverance*, &c. For my *knowing this to be true*, I am cenfured by thofe on *one extream*, as too favourable to the Papifts (being indeed an Enemy to injury, calumny, uncharitablenefs or cruelty to any in the world.) But I am much more difpleafing to the

Roman-party; Because I know, that *One man* is *naturally uncapable* of being the *Monarch of all the world*: That the *King of Rome* (as the *Geographia Nubiensis* calls him) was never by Christ made *King of Kings* and *Lord of Lords*: That he *never was*, nor *can be* a Pastor at the *Antipodes*, and over *all the Earth*, or as far as *Drake* and *Candish* did Navigate: That it's a sorry Argument, [*Monarchy is the best Government*: Ergo, *An universal Monarchy is best*:] That the Government setled in *Nature* and *Scripture*, is for *Princes* to rule *Churchmen and all*, by the *Sword*, and the *Pastors* of all *particular Churches*, to rule their *Congregations* by the *Church-Keys*, that is, by the *Word*, using *Synods* for due *concord* and *correspondency*: And *this much* will do better than all the stir that the *Clergies Ambition* hath made in the world.

I know that the *Pope* standeth on no better a foundation than the *other four Patriarchs*: And that he was but the

chief

chief Prelate or *Patriarch* in *one Empire*, as the Archbishop of *Canterbury* is in *England*; And that the *Greek Church* never took his Primacy in that *one Empire* to be of *Divine Right*: For if they had, they had never *set up the Patriarch of* Constantinople *against him*, *who never claimed his Primacy as jure Divino. I know* that the great Council of *Chalcedon* decreed, Act. 16. Bin. 734. [" We following alwayes the definitions of the " holy Fathers and the Canon, have " our selves also defined the same " things, concerning the Priviledges of " the same Most Holy Church of *Constantinople, New Rome*; For to the Seat " of *Old Rome* because of the Empire of " that City, the *Fathers consequently gave* " the Priviledges: And the one hundred and fifty Bishops most beloved " of God, being moved with the same " intention, have given equal Priviledges to the Most Holy Seat of *New* " *Rome*: Reasonably Judging that the

" City

Chalcedon saith (against Bishop *Bramhall, Survey, pag.* 69.) [*To us it sufficeth, that the Bishop of* Rome *is St.* Peters *Successor; and this all Fathers testifie. But whether he be so* jure Divino vel humano *is no point of faith.* Vid. *Bellarm.* 1. 2. *de Pont. l.* 12. And *Holden Analys. fid. l.* 1. *c.* 9. *p.* 161. *Multa sunt quæ traditione universa firmiter innituntur* (*puta S. Petrum fuisse Romæ*) *quæ revelata non sunt; ideoque ab articulorum fidei Catholicæ numero excluduntur.*

I know that there *never was* such a thing as a *true Universal Council* in the world (unless Christ and his Apostles were such); nor ever *must, or will, or can be.*

I know that they were called *Universal* but as to *one Empire*: and that *Emperours called them* together, who had nothing

thing to *do without that Empire*; and that (unless accidentally any inconsidera-ble number) *no Churches out of the Empire were summoned,* or *sent their Bishops thither*: Which needs no other proof than the knowledge of the *limits* of the *Roman Empire*, and the *Notitiæ Episcopatuum*, and the *Names subscribed* to *each Council* in *Binnius* and the rest.

I know that long ago their *Raynerius* said (*Cont. Waldens. Catal. in Biblioth. Patrum Tom.* 4. *p.*773.) [*The Churches of the Armenians, and Ethiopians, and Indians, and the rest which the Apostles converted, are not under the Church of* Rome.] And that *Godignus* and others make no doubt but the *Abassines* had the faith from the dayes of St. *Matthew* and the Eunuch.

I know that *Theodoret. Histor. Sanct. Patr. c.* 1. saith, [James *the Bishop of* Nisibis *came to the Synod of* Nice; *for* Nisibis *then obeyed the* Roman *Empire.*] Nothing can be more plain.

I know

I know that *Jacob. de Vitriaco* (and others) say (*Hist. Orient. c. 77.*) that [*the Churches of the Easterly parts of* Asia *alone exceeded in number the Christians either of the Greek or Latin Churches*] : And that *Brochardus* that lived at *Jerusalem* saith, that [*those called Schismaticks by us are far better men than those of the* Roman *Church.*]

And to perswade the Kings of *other Kingdoms*, that the necessary *way of Church-Union*, is to unite all their *Subject-Churches* under the *Patriarchs* of *another Empire*, is no wiser than to tell *all the world* that they must be under the *Bishop of* Canterbury.

I know that it was long ere *Our antient Britains*, and especially *Your Scots*, would *so much as eat* with the *Roman* Clergy, (as *Beda* sheweth.)

And *I know* that their *Melch. Canus* saith, (*Loc. Com. cap. 7. fol. 201.*) [*That "not only the Greeks, but almost all the rest "of the Bishops of the whole world, have "fought*

"*fought to destroy the priviledges of the*
"*Church of* Rome ; *And indeed they had*
"*on their side both the Arms of Emperours*
"*and the greater number of Churches: And*
"*yet they could never prevail to abrogate*
"*the power of the One Pope of Rome.*]
Was *this Pope* then (or the *Roman* Church) *Universal?* Besides that, *to this day*, they are but about the third or fourth part of the Christian world.

And I *know* that *General Councils* are *their Religion*: and what the *General approved Council* at *Lateran sub Innoc.* 3. hath Decreed *against Temporal Lords and their Dominions*, *and absolving of their Subjects from their Oaths of Fidelity*: Besides what *Greg.* 7. hath said in his *Concil. Rom.* of his power *to take down and set up Emperours*.

The *knowing* of *these things*, maketh me taken for their enemy. And their *Image of Worship* in an *unknown Tongue*, with their *Bread-Worship* and multitude of *ludicrous deceitful toyes*, are things which

which my ſoul can never be reconciled to: Much leſs to that renunciation of *humanity* which hereafter I detect, in the following Treatiſe.

And having given You this *Account of my ſelf*, I add as to *this Treatiſe*,

1. It grieved me to hear that *ſo many refuſed* the *Parliaments Declaration* againſt *Tranſubſtantiation*: And I deſired to ſhew them *what it is*.

2. Inſtead of joyning with thoſe who *talk much* of the *danger of Popery* in the Land (to keep it out,) I thought it better to *publiſh the Reaſons* which *ſatisfie me againſt it*, and leave the ſucceſs of all to God.

3. And having occaſion to re-print the Firſt Part of my *Key for Catholicks*, with *Corrections*, inſtead of the *Name before prefixed*, (of one whoſe face I never ſaw, nor ever had a word from, but ignorantly endeavoured to have provoked him to do good) I thought *Your Name* fitteſt to be gratefully ſubſtituted,

tuted, who were the *first then* that *checked* my *imprudent temerity*.

Though I was not ſo vain, as to expect of late in your multitude of greater buſineſs, that You ſhould read over my *more tedious* Writings, I deſpair not but You may find leiſure in peruſing *this*, to ſee that I have prefixed Your Name to nothing, but what *Senſe* and *Reaſon* and *Religion* do avow. And ſo Craving Your Pardon for the boldneſs and tediouſneſs of this Addreſs, I reſt,

Your Graces humble much obliged Servant,

August 27. 1673.

Richard Baxter.

[illegible], who were the [illegible] that [illegible]
may [illegible].

Though I was not so vain, as to ex-
pect [illegible] in your multitude of [illegible]
er [illegible], that You should read over
any more [illegible] Writings, I despair not
but You may find leisure in perusing
this, to see what I have prefixed Your
Name to [illegible], [illegible] that Sage and
Religious [illegible]. And to
Learning [illegible] the best [illegible]
[illegible] of this [illegible],

Your [illegible]
[illegible] Servant,

[illegible]

[illegible] Baxter.

TO THE
READER.

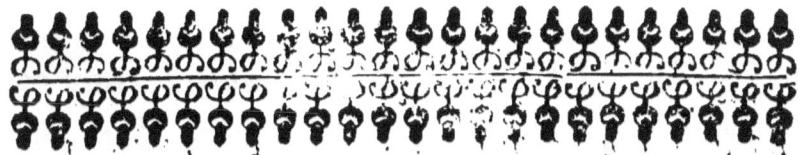

THis Dialogue *cometh not to you, from an apprehension of any extra-ordinary excellency of it, as if it did much more than is already done: but as extorted by mens necessity; 1. Because so many ignorantly turn Papists of late; 2. And some are pleased* to Say (*I dare not say,* To Think) *that it is long of men in my condition; 3. And it is the Art of the Papists (which our vanity encourageth) to seek to bring the old Books into oblivion (which are unanswerable) and to call still for new.*

The intended Use of this is, 1. To tell those that will dispute with a Papist, on what terms and in what order to proceed, lest they be cheated into a snare.

2. *To teach the Ignorant Doubters truly to understand, wherein the difference between us and the Papists doth indeed consist; that the talk of Sectaries Calling that which displeaseth them,* Popery, *nor the scandal of our real or seeming divisions, may not delude them, nor Papists puzzle them by putting them to prove every word in our thirty nine Articles or other Writings.*

3. *To Resolve all that will be Resolved, by* Senses, Reason, Scripture, *or the* Judgement *and Tradition of the Church.*

Of the multitude of Reasons against Popery enumerated, I have here made good but one, by a special disputation; because I would not make the Book too big. The rest I shall easily prove in another Volume, if greater work and shortness of life do not hinder it; (which I fully expect.) And lest I have no more opportunity to answer their Charges aginst us on the other side, I have reprinted and added (Corrected) the first part of my Key for Catholicks, *where it is long ago done, and never answered. There is extant*

one

one Piece of theirs againſt me, unanſwered, called, Mr. Johnſon's Rejoynder *about the* Viſibility of the Church: *which I ſeriouſly profeſs I have left unanſwered, as utterly unworthy of my precious Time, till I have no greater matter to do, which I hope will never be. And he that will well ſtudy his opening of the terms in the latter end, will ſee to how pitiful a caſe they are reduced. I conclude with this ſolemn Profeſsion, That I am ſatisfied of the truth of what I write, and muſt dye ere long in the faith which I here profeſs, and lay my hopes of endleß happineſs on no other way: And that I would joyfully receive any Saving Truth, from Papiſts or any other, who will bring it me, with ſuch evidence as may make it indeed my own. The Lord Unite us by* Truth, Love *and* Humility. *Amen.*

Septemb. 1.
1673.

Richard Baxter.

[illegible] impressions,
Johnson [illegible] hope, and [illegible] from th[illegible]
of the Church. [illegible] I feel
[illegible], as the
[illegible]
[illegible] to [illegible], which I hope I never
that will [illegible] justly [illegible] giving
[illegible] will [illegible] to those
[illegible] reduced. I conclude
[illegible] Profession. That I am sure
truth of what I write, and must
[illegible] which I have professed,
[illegible] of endless happiness on no
[illegible] I would joyfully receive
Truth, from Papists or any others
[illegible] with such evidence as
[illegible] indeed my own. The Lord
Truth, Love and Humility.

Richard Baxter.

THE CONTENTS.

PART I.

PART II.

PART III.

PART IV.

Chap,

ERRATA.

Reader,

I Hope the Printers *Errata* are not many, and I am discouraged from gathering them, because I see men had rather err themselves, and calumniate the Author, than take notice of them: So hath Mr. *Danvers* done by me in a Book against *Infant Baptism*, where as an Introduction to abundance of mistakes in History, he abuseth his Reader by several scraps of a Book of mine, so curtail'd as to be insufficient to signifie the sense; And among them feigneth me to write (*Chr. Direct. p. 3. pag.* 885. *l.* 13. [*to Institute Sacraments*] as that which man may do, instead of [*Not to Institute Sacraments*]; and so maketh his credulous flock to believe that I assert that very thing which I write against: Though the place was markt with a *Star* in the *Errata*, and the Reader *desired* specially to Correct it. But such dealing is now grown so common with such men, that we must bear it as the effect of their disease.

PART. I.

What is the Protestants Religion, and what the Papists.

CHAP. I.

The occasion of the Conference.

D. SIR, I am come to crave your help in a matter of great importance to me: I was bred a Proteſtant; but the Diſcourſes of ſome Roman Catholicks, have brought me into great doubts, whether I have not been all this while deceived: And though I cannot diſpute the caſe my ſelf with you, I deſire you to diſpute it in my hearing with a Catholick Prieſt whom I ſhall bring to you.

R. With all my heart: But let me firſt ask you a few Queſtions.

Queſt. 1. Did you ever underſtand what the Proteſtants Religion is?

D. I take it to be the 39 Articles, Liturgie and Government of the Church of *England.*

R. No wonder if you be eaſily drawn to doubt of that Religion which you no better underſtand. Can you hold it, and not know what it is?

Queſt. 2. Do you know what it is to be a Chriſtian?

D. It is to believe in Chriſt, and to Love and obey Him. Our Baptiſm is our Chriſtening.

R. Very true: And in your Baptiſm you are Dedicated and Vowed to God the Father, Son, and Holy

Ghoſt, renouncing the Luſts of the Fleſh, the World and the Devil.

Queſt. 3. And have you been a true Chriſtian, and lived according to this Vow? Have you obeyed God more than the deſires of your fleſh? Have you preferred the Kingdom of Heaven before all the pleaſures, honours and riches of this world? Have you ſincerely ſubmitted to the healing ſaving Doctrine, Law and example of Chriſt, and to the ſanctifying motions of his Holy Spirit? And have you lived ſoberly, righteouſly, and Godlily in the world, and made it your care and buſineſs to deny your ſelf, and mortifie all fleſhly inordinate deſires, as it is the care of ſenſual men to gratifie them?

D. I have had my faults as all men have; but I hope none can ſay but I have lived honeſtly towards all; And if I have been faulty in drinking, ſports or gaming, it hath been to no ones injury but my own.

R. I ask you not whether you are a *ſinner*; For ſo are all men. But whether you are a *truly Penitent, Converted ſinner*; and whether yet you are *true* to your *Baptiſmal Vow and Covenant?* Can your Conſcience ſay, that you *Love, and Truſt and obey God*, and your *Redeemer*, before all the world; and that you love not Pleaſure, Riches and Honour, more than God and Holineſs and Heaven? and that it is more of the care and buſineſs of your life, to Know and Love and ſerve God better, and to make ſure of your ſalvation, than to pleaſe your fleſh, or proſper in the world? In a word; Do you heartily and in your practice, take God for your God, even for your All, and Christ, for your Teacher, King and Saviour, and the Holy Ghoſt for your Sanctifier,

Johnſ. Nov. Repr. p. 426. Proteſtants formally ſuch, have not enough to be brought to the unfeigned Love of God above all things, and ſpecial Love to his ſervants, and unfeigned willingneſs to obey him: I deny you have any certain knowledge or feeling that you love God or his ſervants, or willingneſs to obey, *&c.*

turning

turning in heart and life, from the Devil, the world, and the sinful pleasures of the flesh? This is the question which I desire you to answer.

But I will prevent your answer lest you mistake my purpose, and think I make my self your Confessour, and I will tell you why I ask the question.

Either you have thus *Kept* your *Baptismal Vow*, by a *Godly life*, or else you have *broken it* by worldliness and sensuality, *&c.* If you have *kept it*, and are a truly *Godly person*, you have resolved your own doubt, and absolutely confuted Popery already. For no honest man and true Christian can possibly turn Papist without gross contradiction.

D. How prove you that.

R. Most easily: I pray you do but mark: 1. It is their principal Doctrine that the Pope is the Head of the Universal Church on earth; and that the Church subjected to him, is the Universal Church; and that out of that Church there is no salvation; and that no one is a true member of Christ and his Church, who is not a subject of the Pope.

2. And they all confess that every one shall be saved that is a true Christian, and keepeth his Baptismal Covenant, and that Loveth God above all. So that they must needs hold that none in the world but Papists, do truly Love God, & keep that Covenant, and are true Christians.

Now if you can know that you have the true Love of God, and are true to your Baptism, you must needs confess that Popery is false, which saith that none Love God above all but Papists.

D. But what if I have not Loved God, and obeyed him, above my flesh?

R. I'le tell you what followeth. 1. It is no wonder if you forsake the Protestants Religion, who never truly entertained it. If your *Heart and Life* were not *de-*

voted unfeignedly to God, you were *no true Christian*, nor indeed had any true Religion at all : And he that hath no Religion, turneth from none which he truly had. If you were never a *true Christian*, you were never a *true Protestant* : And then what wonder if you turn Papist? For you have no *experimental Knowledge* of that Religion which you seem to forsake.

2. And how could you expect better, but that God should penally forsake you, and give you over to believe deceits, if you have dealt so falsly and deceitfully with him, as to live to the world and flesh which you renounced, and neglect that God and Saviour and sanctifier to whom you were so solemnly devoted? And if you have been so treacherous and unwise, as to prefer a bruitish transitory pleasure, before Gods Love and the Joyes of Heaven?

3. And what honour is it to the Church of *Rome*, that none but Infidels and false-hearted hypocrites, and perfidious breakers of their Covenant with God, did ever turn to them ? If you turn Papist, you confess that you were a wicked hypocrite before.

4. But the chief thing which I would tell you is, that turn up and down as oft as you will, to this Church or that Church, to this side or that side, you will never be saved, unless you become a *holy*, *serious*, *mortified Christian* : As long as you love pleasures, wealth and honour more than God and Holiness and Heaven, you shall never be saved, whether you be Papist, or a professed Protestant. It would make the heart of a Christian ake, to see so many thousands cheated by the Devil, to take this opinion or that opinion, called *the true faith*, and this side or that side, called the *true Church*, to be to them instead of a *holy heavenly heart and life*. And how many thousands, especially Papists, that are truly of *no Religion*, do dispute, and plot and disquiet the world,

world, as *for Religion*. To hear a prophane man ſwear that his Religion is right; or that man to think to be ſaved for being of the true Church and *faith*, whoſe heart was never ſet on Heaven, but liveth in drunkenneſs, lying, idleneſs, fornication, and thinketh that the Prieſts abſolution ſets all right again. Without true Holineſs no man ſhall be ſaved, what Church ſoever he joyn with; and with it no man ſhall be damned. For God cannot hate them that have his nature, and Image.

D. Well ſir: I came not to diſpute with you, but to deſire you to meet a Roman Catholick Prieſt, that I may hear you both together.

R. I have the greater hopes of you, becauſe you have ſo much regard of your ſoul, as to be willing to hear what can be ſaid. For moſt that turn to them, never come to an impartial tryal, but raſhly follow the deceiver, or ſtay till they are ſecretly hardened by falſe inſinuations, and then take on them to deſire to hear both, when they are firſt reſolved to be gone.

But you muſt tell me what is the queſtion that you deſire ſhould be diſputed.

D. I would know whether the Papiſts or the Proteſtants be the True, and ſafe Religion?

R. I undertake to give you that plain undenyable evidence for your reſolution, which ſhould fully ſatisfie any reaſonable man, at leaſt that profeſſeth himſelf a Chriſtian: ſo be it you will perform theſe reaſonable conditions: 1. That you will be impartially willing to know the truth. 2. That you will honeſtly reſolve to Live according to it when you know it, and to be True to the True Religion. 3. That you will bring ſuch a man to confer with me, who will yield to the Reaſonable Conditions of a diſputant, ſuch as your Doubt and the nature of the matter doth notoriouſly require, and not a Knave, and ſtudied Deceiver, who will ſet himſelf purpoſely to hide the truth.

D. Theſe conditions are ſo reaſonable that I muſt not deny them.

CHAP. II.

The Conditions of the Conference; between a P. *and* R. *and* D.

R. SIR, I am deſired by this perſon, who is brought by ſome of you to doubt of our Religion, to debate this Caſe with you in order to his ſatisfaction, *Whether the Papiſts or the Proteſtants* be the *True* and *Safe Religion?*

P. That is too large a Queſtion: We cannot diſpute of all our Religion at once: I will begin with you, about ſome one of the Articles of the Church of *England*, or the Viſibility of your Church in all Ages, or the Reſolution of your faith, *&c.* And this I will do only on theſe conditions, 1. That you bring ſome expreſs Text of Scripture, which without your Interpretation, Reaſonings or Conſequences, doth aſſert that Article of yours which I ſhall accuſe, or contradict any Article of our faith, which ſhall be queſtioned. 2. Or if you will go from the expreſs words to Reaſoning, that we keep to the ſtricteſt Rules of Logick, and that you uſe nothing but Syllogiſm, and that all be done in writing, and not by word of mouth.

R. Neighbour *D*. you promiſed me to bring another kind of Diſputant: You hear his conditions: you ſhall hear my anſwer.

1. The Caſe which you told me you were in doubt of, and deſired ſatisfaction in, was *Which is the True*

and

and Safe Religion? This he refuseth to Dispute. Pretending that we cannot dispute of our whole Religion at once. But did you never hear him give any Reasons against our Religion? If he have, Why can he not do it now? I expect not all in a word, but let him give them one by one, and say his worst. I am sure I can give you many against theirs: And we will after debate them particularly as largely as you please.

2. If *Writing* be it that you desire for your satisfaction, I ask you, whether you have read all, or the fourth part, of what is written against Popery already. Have you read Dr. *Challoner* of the Catholick Church? Dr. *White*, Dr. *Field*, Dr. *Downame* of Antichrist, *Chillingworth*, Dr. *Abbot*, Dr. *Willet*, Bishop *Usher*, Bishop *Morton*, Dr. *Stillingfleet*, and an hundred more? Why should I expect that you should read what I shall write, if you will not read what's written already?

3. Can you stay so long unresolved without injury to your soul, till he and I have done writing? You cannot but know, that from Sheets we must proceed to the writing of Volumes, in answering each other, as others have done. And this is like to be many years work, for men that have other business: And how know you that we shall all Live so long?

4. Are you able when it cometh to tedious Volumes to examine them, and find who is in the right? Or will you not rather take him to conquer, who hath the last word? And it's like that will be the longest liver?

5. And as to a strict syllogistical form, do you understand that best? I avoid it not, but shall consent to use it as far as you understand it. Do you know all the Logical forms of arguing, all Moods and Figures, and all the fallacies? Or do you not perceive, that you have broken your promise with me, and brought a

 friend

friend of darkneſs, who cometh purpoſely to hide the truth?

D. I muſt needs profeſs, that the Queſtion which I would have debated, is, *Which is the True and Safe Religion?* And that it is not tedious writings, nor long deſayes, but preſent conference which muſt ſatisfie me. And that it is plain Scripture and Reaſon that muſt ſatisfie me, who underſtand not Logick. I pray let me hear your own *Conditions* which you think more juſt.

R. The Conditions which the nature of the Cauſe directeth us to, are theſe.

I. That we firſt truly ſtate the queſtion to be diſputed: For we cannot diſpute till we are agreed of what: That is, 1. That we agree what we mean by our [*Religion*]; and 2. That I tell you, what is the Religion of Proteſtants, which I undertake to defend: And that he tell us what is the Religion of the Romaniſts, which muſt be compared with it.

II. That our Conference conſiſt of theſe ſeveral parts.

1. That premiſing the principles in which we are agreed, I tell you the Reaſons why you ſhould not be a Papiſt.

2. That he tell you the Reaſons why you ſhould turn Papiſt, or what he hath againſt Our Religion.

3. That then *we* come to diſpute theſe Reaſons diſtinctly: where I will prove *my* charges againſt them, and he ſhall prove *his* charges againſt us one by one.

III. And that in all our diſputes, we ſhall conſent, 1. Not to interrupt each other in ſpeech; but if the length ſeem to overmatch the hearers memory, we will take brief Notes to help our memories, as we go, and crave the recitation of what ſhall be forgotten: For the ſtrength of Truth lyeth ſo much in the connexion of its parts, that when it is mangled into ſcraps by uncivil interterruptions, it is deformed and debilitated and cannot be well understood.

2. That we bind our selves by solemn promise, to speak nothing which we unfeignedly judge not to be truth, nor any thing designedly to hide or resist the truth which we discern.

These terms are so just and necessary, that I will avoid him as a fraudulent wrangler who will deny them. For I come not to scold, nor to try who hath the strongest Lungs, the nimblest Tongue, or the lowdest voice, or the greatest confidence, or fiercest passion; but to try who hath the truth, and which is the true way to Heaven. For the servant of the Lord must not strive; especially about words and barren notions; for that doth but tend to increase ungodliness.

D. Your Method is so reasonable, and so suited to my own necessity, that I must profess no other can so much tend to my satisfaction: And therefore I hope it will not be refused.

(Here after long opposition, the *P.* at last agreeth to these terms).

CHAP. III.

What is the Religion of the Protestants.

R. I. THe word [*Religion*] is sometimes taken *Objectively*; And so I mean by it, [*The objects of Religious Belief, Love and Practice,*] which are, 1. The *Things themselves*; which are the *principal objects* (called by Logicians, The Incomplex terms.) 2. The *organical object*; or the *Revelation* of these Things; containing 1. The *Words* or other *Signs*: 2. The *sense* or *notions* signified.

For

For inſtance, Matth. 17. 5. [*This is my Beloved ſon in whom I am well pleaſed.*] Here 1. The *Real Incomplex object* is *Chriſt Himſelf*, the beloved Son of God, and God the Fathers well-pleaſedneſs in him. 2. The *ſignal* part of the organical object, or Revelation, is the *Words* themſelves, as *ſpoken* then, and written now. 3. The *ſignified notions* are the *Meaning* of the words, and are the chief part of the *organical object*, that is the *Divine Revelation.*

The word [*Religion*] is of larger extent in its ſenſe than [*Faith*]; For it containeth all that Revelation which God hath made Neceſſary to ſalvation; which is twofold, 1. That which is to inform the *underſtanding* with neceſſary *knowledge* and *faith*. 2. That which is neceſſary to a *Holy Will* and a Holy Life, to the Love of God and man, and to well doing; which are Precepts, Promiſes and Threatnings.

II. The word [*Religion*] is oft taken alſo *ſubjectively* (as they ſpeak); For the *Acts* and *habits* of *Love* and *Obedience*.

Now I ſuppoſe we are agreed that it is not *Religion* in this laſt ſenſe that we are to diſpute of (which is as divers as perſons are:) But it is that which we call *Objective Religion*, even the *Organical part* directly. And if by all this *D.* underſtandeth us not, in plainer words, our Queſtion is, *Of the True Divine Revelation*, viz. *Which is the True Rule of Faith, Will and Practice*; that which is held to be ſuch by the Proteſtants: or that which is held to be ſuch by the Papiſts?

T. I grant you, that this is the ſtate of the Queſtion.

R. I here declare to you then, *What is the Religion of the Proteſtants.* IT IS THE LIGHT and LAW OF GOD CONCERNING HOLY KNOWLEDGE and BELIEF, HOLY WILL and PRACTICE,

CON-

CONTAINED IN NATURE and THE TRUE CANONICAL SCRIPTURES.

Here note 1. That our Religion hath its *Essential* parts; And its *Integral* parts and *Accidentals*. I. The *Essentials* of our *Religion*, are contained in the *Baptismal Covenant*; which is expounded in the CREED, the LORDS PRAYER, and the DECALOGUE (as delivered and expounded by *Christ*, and the *Law of Nature*.)

II. Our *Entire Religion*, in the *Essentials*, *Integrals* and *needful Accidentals* is contained wholly in the *Law of Nature* and the *Canonical Scriptures*.

The *Essentials* are delivered down to us two wayes: 1. In *Scripture* with the rest; 2. By the *sure tradition* of the *Universality of Christians*, in *actual Baptizings*, and the *daily profession of Christianity*. This is *all the Protestants Religion*. If you fasten any other on us, we deny it; we own no other. And none know What is *my Religion*, that is, *What I take for the Rule of my holy Faith, Love and Life*, so well as *my self*.

P. This is meer craft: you will make that only which is past controversie among us, to be *Your Religion*, that so your Religion may be past controversie too.

R. It is such Craft as containeth that *naked truth*, which we trust all our own salvation on. I say that *I have no other Religion*; And if you know better than I, disprove me.

P. I disprove you three wayes. I. Because the *Name Protestant* signifieth no such Religion, but somewhat else lately taken up. II. Because the *Augustane Confession*, *the thirty nine Articles* and such like, are by your selves called *The Articles of your Religion*. III. Because all your Writings declare, that besides these, you hold all those *controverted points*, which are *contrary* to that which you call *Popery*.

R. I pray you mark *D.* that he would perswade you that *he knoweth my Religion* better than *I do my self?* What if I should pretend the like as to *his Religion?* Were I to be believed?

P. No: but if you have an odd Religion of your own, that proveth it not to be the *Protestant Religion.*

R. Remember *D.* that *I come not hither to perswade you* to any other Religion, than this which I have mentioned. Let him talk as long as he will what is *other mens opinions, I perswade you to nothing but this,* to take *Gods Law of Nature* and the *Scripture for your Religion.* Either this is *Right* or *Wrong.* If *Right,* fix here and I have done, If *Wrong,* let that be disputed.

But yet I open to you all his three deceits.

I. The name *Protestant* doth not signifie *our Religion,* but our *Protesting* against the *Papists corruptions* and *additions.* I have no Religion but *Christianity: I am a Christian,* and that signifieth *all my Religion.* I am a *Catholick Christian,* that is, of the *Common Christian Faith and Church,* and not of any *heretical dividing Sect:* And I am a *Reformed Protestant Christian,* because *I renounce Popery.* Therefore I rather say [*The Protestants*] than the [*Protestant*] Religion. As if I were among Lepers; If I say; *I am no Leper,* that signifieth not my *Essence:* But if I say, [*I am a Man,* and *I am not a Leper,*] I speak *my Nature,* and *my freedom* from that *disease.* So if I say I am a *Christian Protestant,* I mean only that I am a *Christian,* and *no Papist,* or renouncing *Popery;* as by the word [*Catholick*] I renounce *all Sects and Schisms.* I tell you, *This is my meaning,* when I say, *I am a Protestant,*

Knot against *Chillingworth Ch.* 2. p. 122. [*In no one doctrine Protestants would seem more unanimously to agree, than in this, That all things necessary to salvation are contained evidently in Scripture—which they hold as the only foundation of the whole structure of their Faith and Religion.*] Note this Confession.

Protestant: and can you tell *my meaning* better than *my self?*

II. And as to what he saith of the *thirty nine Articles* and other Church Confessions, I answer, *None of these are our Religion*, in the sense now in question; that is, They are not taken by us to be [*the Divine Revealed-Rule of our Faith, Love and Life*] which is *our Religion* now disputed of. And that this is so, I prove to you past all question.

For 1. Else should we have as *many Religions* as we have *Church Confessions*, and should *alter* our Religion as oft as we alter our *Confessions*; and our Religion should be as *New* as those *Confessions*: All which the Protestants abhor.

2. All those very Confessions themselves do assert that *Gods Word is our only Religion*, and all mens Writings and Decrees are lyable to mistakes: To pass by all the rest, these are the words of our sixth Article, [" Holy Scripture containeth all things Necessary to " salvation: so that whatsoever is not read therein, nor " may be proved thereby, is not to be required of any " man, that it should be believed as an Article of faith, " or be thought Requisite or necessary to salvation]. What would you have more plain and full?

And in the Book of Ordination, it is askt [" Are you perswaded that the Holy Scriptures contain sufficiently all doctrine required of necessity for eternal " salvation? through faith in Jesus Christ? And are " you determined out of the said Scriptures to instruct " the people committed to your charge? and to teach " Nothing (as required of necessity to eternal salvati- " on) but that which you shall be perswaded may be " concluded and proved by the Scripture?] Is not this plain?

P. Why then do you call the thirty nine Articles the

Articles

Articles of your Religion? And what is their uſe? And why are all required to ſubſcribe them?

R. 1. Their Uſe is to ſignifie how the Conjunct Paſtors who uſe them do *underſtand* the Holy Scriptures in *thoſe points*: And that partly for the ſatisfaction of all *forreign Churches*, who may hear us accuſed of Hereſie or Error; and partly to be a hedge to the Doctrine of *young Preachers*, to *keep* them from vending miſtakes in the Churches, and alſo to *try the ſoundneſs* of their underſtandings.

2. The Confeſſions, and Articles, and Catechiſms are *our Religion*, as the Writings of *Perron*, *Bellarmine*, *Suarez*, *&c.* or *many* of theſe *agreeing*, are the *Roman Religion*: They are not the *Divine Revelation and Rule of faith and practice* to us: But they are the *expreſſion* of our *own conceptions* of the *ſenſe* of ſeveral chief matters in that Rule or Revelation. So that they are the *Expreſſion of our faith or Religion taken ſubjectively* (for *acts and habits*) and not our *objective Rule it ſelf*. Our *Sermons* and *Prayers* are our *Religion* in this ſenſe: that is, *The Expreſſion of our own Religious Conceptions*: And ſo are *your Sermons* and *your Writings* alſo to you. But if this were our *Rule of Faith and Life*, and ſo our *Divine Objective Religion*, then we ſhould be of as *many Religions*, as we are *ſeveral perſons*: For every one hath his ſeveral *Expreſſions*: And every new Sermon, or Book, or Prayer, would be a new part of Religion. And ſo with you alſo. So that this doubt is paſt all doubt: Our Confeſſions are but the *expreſſions* of our *perſonal belief*, and not our *Rule of Faith*.

III. And as to your third pretence (that we have other Articles as oppoſite to Popery) I anſwer, *Our Religion* as a *Rule of Faith* and *Worſhip* is *one thing*: And our *Rejecting* all *Corruptions* and *Additions is another.*

ther. *E.g.* My Religion is, that *our God is only the true God*. If now I say also, that *Hercules* is not God, and *Bacchus* is not God, and *Venus*, *Mars*, *Mercury*, *Pallas*, *Neptune*, *Pluto*, *Ceres*, *&c.* are not Gods; is this a *new Religion*, or an *addition* to the former? If the *Baptismal Covenant* be the *Essentials* of my Religion, and the *Creed*, *Lords Prayer and Decalogue* the *Explication* of it; and if the *Scripture* be my *Entire Religion*, and if the Papists will come and add a multitude of *new Articles* and *Corruptions*, my rejecting of those *additions*, is no more an alteration of my Religion, than the sweeping of my house, or the washing of my hands is an alteration of them. So that notwithstanding all that you have said, my Religion is nothing but the *Law of Nature and Scripture*, and my rejecting of Popery, is no otherwise my *Religion*, than my *freedom from the Leprosie*, *&c.* is my *humanity*.

P. Observe, I pray you, that It is no part of your Religion to be against Popery.

R. Observe I pray you, that *Popery* is *against my Religion*, that is, against *much* of the *Christian Religion*; and therefore *my Religion is against Popery*. But I will not quarrell with you about words: When God hath Revealed to us his *Will*, and the Papists add their corrupting inventions, *Gods Revealed Will is my Religion*: your *Corrupting additions* are contrary to it: Call my rejecting such *Corruptions* and *additions*, by the *name* of *my Religion* Reductively (as *Nihil* is *objectum Intellectus*, *&* *Malum Voluntatis*; and as *non-agere* is part of obedience); or Call it *no part of my Religion* in the *primary notion*, but a *Rejecting of its contraries*; so we understand each other I care not.

The truth is, the *Rejecting of some* of your errors, directly contradicting the Scripture it self, may be called *part of our Religion*, as the Negation of the Contrary

trary

trary is included in the ſenſe of an Affirmative: But your *remoter additions*, are contrary to our Religion, but not ſo directly. For inſtance: when the Scripture ſaith, *There is bread after Conſecration*, and you ſay *There is no bread*: My Religion containeth the Aſſertion, that *There is bread*: And ſo includeth a contradiction to your Negative, that ſaith [*There is none*]. Now to ſay, that It is none of my Religion to deny your Negative, who ſay *There is no bread*, would import that It is none of my Religion which affirmeth that *there is bread*. Contradictions cannot both be true: Properly that word that ſaith *There is bread* is my Religion: But this word contradicteth you that ſay *There is none*.

But in another inſtance; my Religion ſaith, that *The Righteous ſhall go into life everlaſting*, and *the reſt to everlaſting puniſhment*; and tells us of a *Heaven and Hell only* hereafter: And you tell us of *Limbus Patrum & Infantum*, and of *Purgatory*: The Scripture enableth us by conſequence to confute this: but if it did not, it were enough for me to ſay, *It is none of my Religion*, becauſe not Revealed by God in *Nature* or *Scripture*; And as it is *your Addition*, ſo to *deny* it, is not *directly* and *properly my Religion* it ſelf, but the *Defence* and *Uſe* of my Religion. God tells us in Scripture, that *He created Heaven and Earth*. If one ſhould aſſert as from God, that God created *ten thouſand Heavens and ten thouſand Earths*, this is a *faith* of his own invention or addition, and it is enough for me to ſay, *I have no ſuch faith*; becauſe God revealeth no ſuch thing. So that ſtill the *Scripture* is the Proteſtants Religion as your *Polydor Virgil* truly deſcribeth them, and others confeſs.

P. All this is meer deluſion: For It is not the *words*, but the *ſenſe* that is *your Religion*; as you will confeſs. And if your Articles or Confeſſions contain a *falſe* a *false sense*, or your Books or Sermons shew that you *falsly expound* the Scripture, your *Religion* is then false.

R. Such Confusion may cheat a heedless hearer: But any one that will take heed, may quickly perceive, that you here fraudulently play with the ambiguity of the word [*Religion*] and quite turn to another question. For you now *speak* of *subjective Religion*, that is, of the *Acts* and *habits* of the *person*: whereas we are disputing only of *objective Religion*, which is *Gods Revelation and our Rule*. If I *understand* any Texts of Scripture amiss, *my faith* is so far defective in *my self*. But *Gods Word*, which is my *Rule*, is never the more imperfect.

I pray you consider how justly you have spoken. 1. Is a mans *Act of faith*, *Gods Word* or *Revelation*? 2. What need you dispute of the *Protestants Religion*, if we have as *many Religions* as *persons*? For it is as certain that we have as many *degrees* of our *understanding many Texts* of Scripture? 3. Would not this prove also as *many Religions* as *persons* among *your selves*? Is it not most certain that no two Papists in the world, have just the same sense or conceptions of the *Scriptures* and *Councils* in *each particular*. The *Law of God* is my only Religion, *objectively*, as now disputed of: If I *mistake* any *essential* part of it, so as to deny it, I am *personally a Heretick*: If I mistake any *Integral* part, I so far err from the *Rule* of my *Religion* or *faith*. But I still profess, that I take Gods *Word* or *Law* only for my sure unchangeable *Rule* or *objective Religion*, and I am daily learning to understand it better, and as soon as I see my error I will reform it, and blame *my self* and not *my Rule*. And I think you will say the same of *your Rule* and of *your personal errors*.

P. This shall not serve your turn: For every Law must have its *promulgation* : And if it be not *manifested* to you that Scripture is Gods Law, and sufficient, it cannot be *your* Rule: I ask you therefore,

Qu. 1. Is it the Scripture in the *Original*, or in the *Translations*, which you say is your *Religion*, *Law* or *Rule?*

R. I told you our Divine Rule consisteth of *Words* and *Meaning*. It is only the *Originals* which are our *Rule* or *Religion* as to the very *words*; that is, Only the *Original words*, were of that *Divine Inspiration*. But every *Translation* is so far *Gods Word*, in *sense*, as it expresseth truly the *sense* of the *original words*.

P. *Qu*. 2. I pray you what then is the Religion of all the unlearned Protestants, who know not a word of the *Originals?* They may see now that you have stript them of all *Divine Religion*.

R. Their Religion is the same *objectively* with that of the most learned, as *delivered from God*; but it is not *equally learned* and understood by them; *Gods Word* in the *Original Tongues* is given them as the *Rule* of *Faith* and *Worship*; and *Teachers* are appointed to help them to understand it. When these *Teachers* have *Translated* it to them, they have the *same sense*, though not the *same words*, for their Religion. And to know the *Words* is not so necessary to salvation, as to know the *sense* (or sentence) though by *other words*: For the *words* are but *means* to know the *Sense*; and the *sense* but a *means* to know the *Things*, (*viz*. God, Christ, Grace, Glory, &c.) And as they have the *same God*, *Christ*, *Spirit*, *Grace*, *Glory*, &c. to be the *real objects* of their Religion, so have they the same *Do-Doctrine* and *Law* in *sense* which is in the Originals.

P. *Q*. 3. And I pray you, How shall the unlearned

be sure that the Translations are true as to the sence? when you have no Divine Infallible Translators?

R. I also ask you. 1. How was all the Greek Church for many hundred years sure of the soundness of the Translation called the Septuagint? or that of *Aquila, Theodot. Symmachus, &c.* when it is certain that in many things they were all unsound?

2. How was the *Latine Church* sure of the soundness of *their Translation* before *Hierome* amended it? And how have you been sure *since then*, when Pope *Sixtus*, and Pope *Clement* have made so many hundred alterations or differences? Had you then *Infallible Translators?* And why then do your Translators (as *Montanus* and others) still differ from that *Vulgar Latine?*

3. And how do all your unlearned persons know that you give them not only the *true sence* of the *Scriptures*, but of *all your Councils* or *Traditions?*

But I will answer you directly. We still distinguish the *Essentials* of our *Religion*, from the *Integrals* and *Accidentals*. 1. The *unlearned* may be *certain* that the *Essentials* are truly delivered them in *sence*: Because they have them not *only in the Scripture*, but by *Universal certain Tradition*, in the *constant Use of Christian Baptism*, and in the *use of the Creed, Lords Prayer and Decalogue* in all the Church-assemblies: And they may easily know that mens tempers, Countreys, *Interests, opinions* in other points, and sidings are so various, that it is not a thing possible without a miracle, that all these should conspire both in a *false Translation*, and *Universal assertion* and *Tradition* of all these *Essentials*. For the effects must be contrary to a torrent of Causes: The Papists, Protestants, Arians, Greeks, Socinians, Lutherans, Calvinists, Anabaptists, Separatists, *&c.* have so much animosity against each other, that undoubtedly if any party of them did falsifie Scripture even in the *Essentials* which are easily discerned, multitudes would quickly detect it and contradict them. And this the *unlearned* may surely and easily discern.

But as for all other *less necessary texts* of Scripture, neither *you* nor *we*, *learned* or *unlearned*, are *certain* that they are *perfectly translated*, nor are they by any one *perfectly understood*, nor are they sure (by reason of the *various readings*) which *copie* of the original is *absolutely faultless*.

2. But suppose that an unlearned weak Believer were not absolutely *certain* (as he may be) that the very *essentials of Christianity* are truly opened to him, he may yet grow up to better understanding, and he may be saved with *some doubtings* of *Christianity* it self, so be it his Faith be *more prevalent* than those doubtings, upon his Heart and Life.

P. Is it a safe Religion which you your self describe? When no man can be sure that he rightly understandeth all the Scriptures? and when your believer is uncertain, even of Christianity it self? Let *D*. Judge whether this be a sure Religion.

R. The word of God is *absolutely certain in it self*; but that so much uncertainty may be in *believers*, I will make you to your shame confess your self, and recant these insinuations.

Q. 1. Dare you say that *all your Church*, or *any one man*, even the *Pope himself*, doth understand *all the Scripture*? or *can perfectly* and *infallibly translate each word*? You dare not say it. Else why did he never once pretend to give us either an unerring Commentary or Translation? And why have you such great diversity of both?

Q. 2. How much less dare you say that any of you perfectly understand *all the Councils*, which are the rest of your Religion? No nor that you have *certainty*

which

which are the *true Copies* of them all? else why do *Caranza, Crab, Surius, Binnius, Nicolinus, &c.* give give us such various Copies? And yet you confess the *Scriptures* to be *Gods word*, and with the *Councils* to contain *your Religion.*

Q. 3. If God have *promised salvation*, to all that truly hold and practise the *Essentials* (the *Baptismal Covenant*) doth the difficulty of other points (in Genealogie, Chronologie, History, by-matters) either make our *salvation* ever the *less certain*, or any way impeach the word of God? What disgrace is it to a man that besides *Head* and *Heart*, he hath fingers, and toes, and nails and hair? No more is it to the Scripture, that as our *entire Religion*, it containeth even *Integrals* and *Accidentals.*

Q. 4. And as to a *Doubting Believer*, I ask, Dare you say that all those were Infidels or in a state of damnation, who said, *Lord increase our faith?* or *Lord we believe; help our unbelief?* or to whom Christ said, *Why are ye afraid O ye of little faith?* or that said, Luk. 24. *We trusted that this had been he that should have delivered Israel?* Or if a man should *doubt* even of the *Life to come*, and yet his *Faith* be so much more powerful than his *doubts*, as that he resolveth to *prefer* his *hopes of Heaven* before all *this world*, and to seek it on the most self-denying terms, even to the laying down of life it self, are you *sure* that this *man shall be damned?* But this is the Course of pievish wranglers. To maintain their own opinions and put a face of *certainty* on their own conclusions, they stick not to damn almost all the world. For it will be no less, if all *doubting believers* must be damned.

See the Roman *Catech.* where this is confest, *Cap.* 1. *q.* 1. pag. 9.

5. It

5. It is a grofs delufion to pretend that there is a neceffity, that *All Gods Infallible word*, muft needs be taught us by as *Infallible Infpired Prophets* or other perfons, as thofe that firft delivered it. *Tranflation* is but the *firft part* of *expofition*, And muft we have none but *Infallible* or *Prophetical Expofitors*?

See Dr. *Holden Anal f. fidei* Li. 1. c. 3. Lett. 1.

6. Is it *All the Scriptures*, or but *fome part*, that your Pope or Councils can *Infallibly* both tranflate and expound? If *but fome*, we need not their Infallibility or Infpiration, for the *moft plain* and *neceffary* parts: It is and can be done without them. If it be *All*, how impious and cruel are they that would never do it to this day?

7. And why ufe all your Expofitors the common helps of Grammars, Lexicons, Teachers, long ftudies, and yet differ *de fide* (even of the fenfe of many a text of Scripture) when all is done, if your Pope have the gift of Infallible Tranflating and expounding all?

P. Remember that your felves derive your *Effentials* from *Tradition*.

R. Yes, and our Integrals to: What objective prefence to the fenfes, (eyes and ears) of thofe that heard Chrift and his Apoftles, and faw their miracles was to the firft Converts in thofe times, that partly *Tradition* is to us, or the neceffary *medium*. The *words* could not come down to us, without fome to deliver them. We have the *Bible* by *Tradition*, and we have *practical Tradition of Baptifm* and the *Creed* by *it felf*, and that in many languages; where we are fure we have all the *neceffary fence*. But do you remember that this is

He that would know what ftrefs we lay on Tradition as the Medium may fee it fully in my *Reafons of Chrift. Relig.* And Dr. *Holden* is more for us than for the Papifts, *Cap.* 3.

Uni-

Universal Tradition, and not *meer Roman Tradition*; such as is *certain* by *moral Evidence*, even the *consent of all* that are yet of *cross opinions and Interests*, (as to matter of fact); *Historical Evidence*; and not the pretended *certainty of a Pope* and his *favourites*, phanatically claiming a spirit of Infallibility.

But I am not now disputing with you, I am only telling you that the *Protestant Religion* is *nothing but Christianity and the Scriptures.* And all our *Confessions* are our Religion (besides *Consent*) but as our *Sermons* and *Treatises* are, which vary as they are various expressions of mens various subjective faith; while *Gods word* varyeth not.

P. If the *Bible* be your Religion, then the Ceremonial Law of *Moses* is your Religion: For that is part of the Bible.

R. You study what to say against another, and never think how it concerneth your selves. 1. Is not the *Bible* at least *Part* of *your* Religion? You dare not deny it. And is the *Ceremonial Law* of *Moses* therefore *your Religion?*

2. I told you that as a *perfect man* hath *hair* and *nails*, which are but *Accidents*, so the *Bible* hath more than the *Integrals* of our Religion.

3. The *Ceremonies* of *Moses* in that sense as now they are delivered to us in the Bible, are *parts* or *appurtenances* of our Religion: That is, the *historical narrative* of those *Abrogated Laws*, which now bind us not as Laws, but tell us (as the Prophesies) what *was heretofore*, and how Christ was fore-typified, and what intimations of Gods will we may gather from the history. And the abrogated Laws are no otherwise delivered to us, and so we must use them.

P. If the ten Commandments be your Religion, you must keep the Jewish seventh day Sabbath:

So that neither there can you fix.

R. The same answer will serve. 1. The ten Commandments are no otherwise part of *our Religion* than they are of *yours.* 2. They are a *Law to us*, as delivered and expounded by *Christ*, and in *Nature*: and the seventh day is an abrogated part of *Moses* Law.

P. If the *Creed* be your Religion, you must take the Article of Christs descent into Hell to be necessary to salvation.

R. 1. Is the *Creed* no part of *your* Religion? As you answer, so may we. 2. I did not tell you that the Creed had *no more* than the *Essentials.* I told you that all the *Essence* of Christianity is in the *Baptismal Covenant*: And he that understandeth *that*, understandeth *it all.* And that the *Creed*, the *Lords Prayer*, and the *Christian Decalogue* are the *exposition* of it. But the Exposition may have *somewhat more* than the *Essentials.* 3. The *Creed* was not written first in English, nor Latine; And Christs descent to *Hades* is more needful to be believed, than his descent to *Hell*, as the word is commonly taken in English.

But, to conclude, remember, 1. That I profess here to own and plead for *no other Religion* (as we explained the word) but *Gods Law* of *Nature and Scripture.* 2. That I profess to perswade D. to no other: And you cannot make me a Religion against my will.

CHAP.

CHAP. IV.

What is the Papists Religion.

R. I Have plainly told you what my own, and the Protestants Religion is, viz. [*Nothing but Christianity*; *contained Integrally in the holy Scriptures*; *And the* Essentials *being the* Baptismal Covenant, *explained in the Creed, Lords prayer and Christian Decalogue, are delivered to us both in the said* Scriptures, *and by* distinct Tradition; *which also hath brought down to us the* Scripture it self: *Not a Tradition depending on the pretended* Authority of the Roman Pope *or* party, *or on any other that shall pretend the like*; *But that* Historical Evidence *of* matter of fact, *which is* surelier *given us by* all sorts of Christians, *taking in the Concord of many Hereticks, Infidels and Enemies*; *which* evidence *dependeth not on the credit of* supernatural Revelation, *but on the* natural credibility *yea and* certainty *of such* universal Circumstantiated Concordant testimony; *and is necessarily antecedent to the Belief of* supernatural Revelations *in the particulars, as* sight *and* hearing *were in the auditors of Christ and the Apostles*; *seeing these two Acts of Knowledge*, [Whatever God saith is True; *and* This God saith] *must necessarily go before our* Belief *or* Trust *that* [This is True, because God saith it.] *And so we run not in a circle, and need not a supernatural faith, for the founding of our first supernatural faith*; *that is, A first before the first.*]

Without fraud or obscurity this *is our* faith and Religion.

Now do you as honestly and plainly tell me *What is Yours*, which *D.* must be perswaded to: For I confess that

that I take it to be an *unintelligible* thing, and despair that ever you give any man a certain notice, what it is, which may be truly called the Religion of your Roman-Catholick-Church.

P. I shall make you understand it if you are willing: But 1. Note that [*Religion*] being a larger word than [*faith*] includeth also [*Practice*] or [*Manners*], we must give you a distinct account of each: For they have not the same Causes: Our *Faith* is *Divine*; But our *Manners* or *Practice* must follow the *Laws* of the *Church*, as well as the Immediate Laws of God: These must not be confounded.

R. Man hath three faculties, *Intellective*, *Volitive* and Vitally-*Executive*, or *Active:* Our *Religion subjectively* must be in all, *viz.* The Sanctity of all, by Holy *Life*, *Light* and *Love:* And therefore the *Rule* which is our *objective Religion* doth extend to all, (to *Intellect*, *Will and Practice*). And surely for *All*, there is a *Rule directly Divine*, given by *Inspiration* of the *Holy Ghost* or Christs own words, and *subordinate Rules* by *Christs Ministers*, which are directly *Humane*, and no otherwise *Divine* than as God hath in General authorized them thereto. Even as the *Soveraign* hath the only *Universal Legislative power*, and *Magistrates by Him* are authorized to subordinate *mandates* and acts of Government. And so we have a *Divine Faith* and *Revelation*, and a *subordinate Humane faith* and Ministerial Revelation or Preaching: We have *Divine Perswasions*, and *subordinate Perswasions* of *men*: We have *Divine Laws*, yea and *executions*; and we have *Humane subordinate Laws* and *executions*. If you resolve to call the *Humane*, *Divine* so far as they are indeed *Authorized* by God, I will not quarrel about words: But remember, 1. That so you must do also on the same reasons, by the *Laws* of *Kings* and the Commands of *Parents*,

Parents, who are as much authorized by God to their proper Government. 2. And I hope you mean not to Confound these *Humane Laws*, with *Gods own Universal Laws*, nor *humane faith* with *Divine faith*. And be it known to you, It is the *Divine Revelations* and *Laws as distinct from the Humane*, which we are now calling our *Religion*, and disputing of; though this Religion teach us to obey *Parents*, *Pastors* and *Princes*, and that obedience may be consequentially and reductively called *Religious* if you please. But if really your *Religion* be not *Divine*, but *Humane*, let us know it. For by the word [*Religion*] we essentially mean that which is [*Divine*.]

P. Men were the speakers and writers of the Scriptures, and so far they are humane, as well as the Decrees of the present Church.

R. The Decalogue was witten by God, and delivered by the Ministry of Angels: Christ was owned by a Voice from Heaven. And himself spake and did most recited by the four Evangelists: And the Prophets and Apostles spake by the immediate Infallible Inspiration of the Holy Ghost: So that the Holy Ghost is the Author of the Scriptures. But the present Pastors of the Church instead of that Immediate Revelation from God by the Spirits Inspiration, have but the ordinary help of the Spirit, to understand those same Revelations, and that proportioned to the measure of their *diligence*, *natural parts* and *helps of Art*, as the knowledge of Theologie is attained by other Students; who are none of them perfect or free from error.

P. I will tell you what our Religion is, *It is Gods Word concerning things to be Believed and Done delivered partly in the Canonical Scriptures, and partly by*

Oral

Oral Tradition, and *received by the Church*, and *by it delivered to us*. The *Trent. Catech. Prefac. q.* 12. saith, *Omnis doctrinæ ratio, quæ fidelibus tradenda sit, verbo Dei continetur, quod in Scripturam, Traditionesq; distributum est. The Reason of every doctrine which is to be delivered to the faithful, is contained in the Word of God, which is distributed into the Scripture and Traditions.*

Q. Was it from the Church that the first Church received it? Or was it not the same Divine Religion which the first Church (whether Council or Practicers) received without the Tradition of Council or Practicers? If so, this cannot be essential to Religion. If the Apostles words were to be believed, their proved Writings are to be believed. And their Writings were proved theirs before a General Council or Universal Practice witnessed it: Even by each Church and person that received any Epistle from any one of them.

Vide Concil. Senonens. in Bin. Decr. 5. p. 671. & Concil. Tridentini Sess. 4. p. 802. — *Perspiciensque hanc Veritatem & disciplinam contineri in libris sacris, & sine scripto Traditionibus, quæ ex ipsius Christi ore ab Apostolis acceptæ, & ab ipsis Apostolis Spiritu sancto dictante quasi per manus traditæ, ad nos usque pervenerunt, orthodoxorum patrum sententiam sequuta, omnes libros tam Veteris quam Novi Testamenti, nec non Traditiones ipsas, tum ad fidem, tum ad mores pertinentes, tanquam vel ore tenus a Christo, vel a Spiritu sancto dictatas, & continua successione in Ecclesia Catholica conservatas, pari pietatis affectu & reverentia suscipit ac veneratur.*

Bellarmin. de Verbo Dei, lib. 4. *c.* 2, 3. sheweth the divers sorts of unwritten Traditions which are part of Gods Word: some *de fide*, as *the perpetual Virginity* of *Mary*, *that there are but four Gospels, &c.* and some of Manners; as *Crossing, Fast-dayes, &c. Easter, Whitsontide*, and other Festivals.

Veron

Veron de Reg. fid. cap. 2. saith, [" The total and " only Rule of the Catholick faith, to which all are " obliged under pain of Heresie and Excommunication, " is *Divine Revelation delivered to the Prophets and " Apostles, proposed by the Catholick Church in her* " General Councils, or by her Universal practice, to " be believed as an Article of Catholick faith.] ["All " that is of this nature is an Article or doctrine of " faith. And no other doctrine can be of faith, if " either the first Condition fail, viz. *Divine Revelati-" on, or the second*, which is a Proposal by the Uni-" versal Church.] p. 5. No doctrine grounded on " Scripture *diversly interpreted*, either by the antient " Fathers or our Modern Doctors, is an Article of faith. " For such a doctrine, though it may be revealed, yet " the revelation is not ascertained to us, nor proposed " by the Church: ——— " Nor any Proposition which " can be proved only by con-" sequence drawn from Scri-" pture, though the con-" sequences were certain and " evident, and deduced from two propositions of Scri-" pture ——— Yet these doctrines are Certain, when " the premises are so. —— *Gratians* decrees — the " Papal decrees contained in the body of the Canon " Law, none of them do constitute an Article of " faith ——— Nor that which is defined in Provin-" cial Councils, though the Pope preside in person —— " for the second condition is alwayes wanting in this " case, and very often the first ——— *p.* 11. I did not " say that such definitions " were not *of faith* ——— " but they are not of *Catho-" lick faith*, or which all as Catholicks are bound " to

So that if the Doctors will but differ in their Expositions, the Scripture is no more the sure Word of God, or to be believed by Catholick faith.

Of the Pope without a General Council.

"to hold as of faith, and the contrary to which is "heretical, and removeth from the boſome of the "Church.——*p.*12, 13. The "*Practice* even of the *Universal Church* is no ſufficient ground for an Article of Catholick faith; "by reaſon the object of faith is *Truth*: and "oft times the Church proceeds in matter of *practice*, "upon *probable Opinions*, and this *probability* is ſufficient to juſtifie the *practice*, which the Church on "juſt cauſe may change: As *e.g.* as *Vaſquez* teacheth, the Church did antiently pray in the Maſs for "Infidels alive, and Catechumens dead, and the Sacrifice of the Maſs was offered for them, and yet he "—— rather inclineth to the contrary, that the Sacrifice of the Maſs ought not to be offered, but for the "faithful living and dead, by which Opinion the "Church ſeemeth guided at preſent. But *Vaſquez* "anſwers, that the Church following a probable opinion did practiſe that which ſhe did not declare to "be of faith.———*p.* 15. So General Councils "when they mention any thing in this manner (by way "of ſimple aſſertion) and do not properly *define*: "For as *Bellarmine* affirms, it is neceſſary that General Councils *properly define* the thing in queſtion, as "a *Decree* which *ought to be held as of Catholick* "*faith*. Hence *Bellarmine* adds, they are not properly *Hereticks*, who hold the Pope not to be above all "Councils, though he ſay the laſt *Laterane* Council "under *Leo* the tenth *Seſ.* 11. expreſly and profeſſedly "teacheth that the Pope is above all Councils, and "rejects the contrary Decree of the Council of *Baſil*: "because it is *doubtful* whether the *Laterane* Council "defined that doctrine *properly* as a Decree to be *be-*

Mark then, that it may be *de fide divina*, though not of *catholick neceſſity* without the propoſal of Council or univerſal practice.

"*leived*

" *lieved with Catholick faith.* The same *Bellarm. (de* " *Concil. l. 2. c. 19.)* also requireth that the definition " be made *Conciliarly*: Pope *Martin* the fifth said, he " only confirmed those Decrees of faith which were " made in the Council of *Constance*, *Conciliariter*: " that is, after the manner of other Councils, the que- " stion being first diligently examined: But its clear " (saith he) that this Decree, that a General Council " hath immediate authority from Christ, which all, " even the Pope, are bound to obey, was made without " any *examining*—*p.* 17. The object defined must " be truly and properly an object of faith; and a " Decree ought to be on a thing universally proposed " to the whole Church———*Vasquez* holds: It is " not at all erroneous to affirm that a General Coun- " cil may err in Precepts, and in particular Judge- " ments———and *(p. 19.)* in framing Laws not " necessary to salvation; or making superfluous Laws--- " Without all doubt a General Council may err in a " question of fact: (which depends on testimony and " information of men:) So the sixth General Council " condemned *Honorius* of Heresie by false Information, " and misunderstanding his Epistles. ——— *p.*20. The " Pope (saith *Suarez*) to a particular action belonging " to humane Prudence, hath no infallible assistance of " the Holy Ghost——As that such or such an excom- " munication is valid, or that such or such a Kingdom " is disposable by the Pope for such and such causes.] So *far Veron*, who is most favourable to you, in narrowing our faith.

R. Thus far you have resolved me: but I must crave somewhat more. *Qu.* I. Are there no Essential Constitutive parts of your Religion, more necessary than the *Integrals* and *Accidentals*? Have you no description for it, but that *It is Divine Revelation proposed by the*

the Church? The *Doctrine* of *Sacrificing* was a *Divine Revelation* to *Adam*, and the difference of *clean and unclean Beasts* to *Noah*, and the Jewish Law was *Gods Revelation* to *Moses* and them: And yet I suppose Christianity is somewhat different from all these. Is not *Christianity* your Religion? Hath *Christianity* no *Constitutive special Essence*, but only the *Genus of Divine Revelation* which is common to that with all other *Divine Revelations?* And what if you add [*to a Prophet or Apostle*]? Was *Agabus* Prophesie of *Paul*, or *Pauls* of the event of the shipwrack, *&c.* essential to *Christianity?* Hath Christianity no *Essence?* Or is all *Divine Revelation essential* to it?

P. You take advantage of the disagreement of our Doctors. You know that some few acknowledg *distinct fundamentals*; and some deny the distinction in your sense: And most of us say, that no man can enumerate the things necessary to all, but that it dependeth upon mens various capacities, educations, and means of knowing. And in sum, that no more is necessary to all to be *explicitly* believed, but that *Gods Revelations are true*; and that *All are Gods Revelations which the Church proposeth as such.*

Johns. Nov. Rep. p. 19. of the explication of Terms: *Know you not, that Divines are divided, what are the points necessary to be believed explicitely* necessitate medii: *Some, and these the more antient hold, that the explicite belief of God, of the whole Trinity, of Christ, his Passion, Resurrection,* &c. *are necessary* necessitate medii: *Others among the recentiors, that no more than the belief of the Deity, and that he is the rewarder of our works, is absolutely necessary with that necessity, to be explicitely believed.*

You may take our judgement much from him that cometh nearest to you, whom I have heard you much praise, as most moderate and judicious, *viz.* Dr. *H. Holden Anal. fid. l.* 1. *c*, 5. *Lect.* 2. *p.* 53. [" Divines " disputing of the necessity of points to be believed, do " commonly tend this way, to denote the Articles of " thing

" things revealed, the explicite and express belief
" whereof, is (as they opine) altogether necessary to
" all Christians. The resolution of which question is
" among them so doubtful and uncertain, as that they
" are in this (as ☞ *they are in all things else*) di-
" stracted and divided into various Opinions: which
" they that care for them, may seek: To me they are
" as Nothing, while the Authors of them profess, that
" they have nothing of Certainty. Yea, to one that
" meditateth the matter it self, laying by all preoccu-
" pation, it is most clearly manifest, that the Resolution
" of this question is not only *unprofitable*, that I say not
" *pernicious*, (as it is handled by Divines); but also vain
" and impossible. It is unprofitable, because no good ac-
" crueth by it to souls. ☞ It is pernicious, while Divines
" for the most part assert, that only *One* or *Two Arti-*
" *cles*, yea, (as some say) no singular Article at all, is
" necessary to be believed of all by an explicite faith:
" For hence (however the truth of the matter be)
" the colder Christians taking occasion, do little care
" to obtain that degree of Knowledge in the Mysteries
" of faith, which they might commodiously and easily
" attain. It is *Impossible*, seeing it is Manifest, that no
" particular Rule or Points to be believed, or Number
" of Articles can in this Matter be given or assigned,
" which shall be wholly common and necessary to all
" Christians: For this dependeth on every individual
" mans natural capacity, means of instruction, and all
" the other circumstances of each mans life and dispo-
" sition, which are to each man so special, that we can
" determine of nothing at all that is common to all.

" But I handle the Necessity of points to be Believed
" in a far other sense: For the Articles of the Christi-
" an faith, which I now call necessary, I do not at all
" understand to be such as all and every one must di-

"stinctly know, or hold by explicite assent ; But I "mean only such, the belief of which is accounted "universally by the whole Catholick Church, so sub-"stantial and essential, as that he that will deservedly "be esteemed, and truly be a member of it, must needs "adhere to them all at least "Implicitely and Indirectly : "that is, by believing whatsoever the holy and Univer-"sal Church doth Catholickly believe and teach as a "Revealed Doctrine and Article of divine faith. And "therefore he is for that cause to be removed from "its Communion and Society, who shall pertinaciously "and obstinately deny the least of them, much more "if he maintain the contrary, while he *knoweth* and "*seeth* that it is the Universal sentence of that Church, "that we must adhere to that as an Article of faith. And "in this sense I will henceforth use the word *Necessity*.

He doth better interpret the distinction of Explicite and Implicite on another occasion, in another sense.

R. This might have been said in fewer and plainer words, *viz*. That your Divines herein do commonly err, and that perniciously, and yet that indeed he is of the same mind; *viz*. that It is impossible to name the Articles necessary to be believed explicitely of all, because each mans divers capacity, means and circumstances diversifie them to each : But that only this one thing is explicitely to be believed, [That whatsoever the Holy and Universal Church doth Catholickly believe and teach as a Revealed Doctrine and Article of faith, is true.] And therefore that no man must pertinaciously deny any thing which he knoweth the Church so holdeth. So that nothing is necessarily to be believed actually and indeed, but *Gods* and the *Churches Veracity*.

P. Another of ours that cometh as near you as most, openeth this more fully, *Davenport* aliàs *Fr. a*

"*Sancta*

Sancta Clara, De. Nat. Grat. p. 111, *&c.* [" As to
" the Ignorance of those things that are of necessity of
" Means, or End, there is difference among the Do-
" ctors: For *Soto* 4. *d.* 5. *q.* 5. *& l. de Nat. & Grat.*
" *c.* 12. *& Vega l.* 6. *c.* 20. *sup. Trid.* hold that now
" in the Law of Grace there is no more explicite faith
" required, than in the Law of Nature. Yea, *Vega ib.*
" *& Gabriel* 2. *d.* 21. *q.* 2. *ar.* 3. *&* 3. *d.* 21. *q.* 2. think
" that in the Law of Nature, and in Cases in the Law of
" Grace, some may be saved with only natural know-
" ledge, and that the habit of faith, is not re-
" quired. Whom *Herantius* terms men of great name,
" and will not accuse of heresie. I would this great
" mans modesty were more frequent with modern Do-
" ctors. Yea, *Alvarez de aux. disp.* 56. with others,
" seemeth to hold, that to justification there is not at
" all required the knowledge of a supernatural object
" (or the supernatural knowledge of the object.)
" Others hold, That both to Grace and Glory is re-
" quired an explicite belief of Christ. *Bonav.* 3.
" *d.* 25, *&c.* Others, that at least to salvation is an
" explicite belief of the Gospel or of Christ, though
" not to Grace or Justification. And this is common
" in the Schools, as *Ferera* shews that followeth it:
" And for this Opinion *Scotus* is cited — But I think he
holdeth, that explicite belief of Christ or the Gospel, is
" not of necessity of means as to Grace or Glory, as
" 4. *d.* 3. *q.* 4. What is plainer than that now —
" men may be saved without the explicite belief of
" Christ ——— And I plainly think its *Scotus*'s and
" the common opinion, which *Vega* followeth, and *Fa-*
" *ber* 4. *d.* 3. and *Petigianis* very well, and of the
" Thomists *Bannes* 2. 2. *q.* 2. *a.* 8. *Canus* and others: Yea,
" the *Trent* Council seemeth to favour it, *Sess.* 6. *c.* 4.
" —— *p.* 114. So *Corduba, Medina, Bradwardine.* ——

" ☞ *And such* (as have no explicite faith in Christ)
" *are not formally without the Church.* This way go
" *Victoria in 4. Relect. 4. tit. Richard de Villa med.* 3.
" 25. *a.* 3. *q.* 1, *&c.*

" Well saith *Petigianis* 2. *d.* 35. *q.* 1. *a.* 9. that if
" there were a simple old woman to whom some false
" Opinion were preached by a false Prophet (*e.g.* that
" the substance of Bread remaineth with the body of
" Christ in the Sacrament) and she believe it: Doth
" she sin by this? No.———*p.* 119. Yea, if she so
" err through piety, thinking that the Church so be-
" lieveth, perhaps she should merit.———*p.* 120. For
" my part I think that the Vulgar committing themselves
" to the instruction of the Pastors, trusting of their
" knowledge and goodness, if they be deceived, it will
" be taken for invincible ignorance, or at least pro-
" bable, (as *Herera*) which excuseth from faulti-
" ness.———Yea, some Doctors give so much to the
" Instruction of Pastors, that have the care of the
" Sheep, that if they should teach, that ☞ *hic &*
" *nunc* God would be hated, the rude Parishioner were
" bound to believe him: which yet I think false——
" *p.* 123. It seemeth at this day to be the common
" judgement of the Schools and Divines, that the Laity
" erring with their Doctors or Pastors are altogether
" excused from all fault; ☞ Yea, oft times so mate-
" rially erring do merit for the act of Christian obedi-
" ence which they owe their Pastors: as you may see
" in *Valent. To.* 3. *disp.* 1. *q.* 2. *p.* 5. and others. So
" *Angles* 2. *d.* 22. *q.* 2. *dub.* 7. *Vasqu. p.* 2. *disp.* 121.
" In case they never doubted of the Veracity of their
" Prelates.

Much more saith *Sancta Clara* there, to prove that the ignorant Protestants here may be saved; citing further to his end, *Zanchez in Decal. l.* 2. *c.* 1. *n.* 8. *Alph.*

a Castro, *Simanca*, *Argon*, *Tanner*, *Faber*, *Eman.sa*, *Rozell*. And out of *Argon* tells us when Faith is sufficiently proposed, *viz*. [" When faith is so confirmed " by Reasons, holiness of life, the confutation of the " contrary errors, and by some signs, as that Reason it " self beginneth prudently to prescribe, that the mat-" ters of faith heard are to be believed, and the con-" trary Sect is false.] *p*. 125.

" And *probl*. 16. *p*. 127. Whether men may be " blamelesly ignorant of the Law of Nature and the " Decalogue? The common opinion is that they may; " not of the first principles, but 1. Of the easie conclu-" sions for some time, and of the remoter conclusions " for a longer time: Such are the Commandments of " the Decalogue as to the substance of the act; as in " some lying, theft, fornication, manslaughter (in Will " at least) *&c*.

R. *Qu*. II. But do you think that men may not as invincibly and inculpably be unacquainted with the Authority of the Pope and *Roman* Councils or Church, as you say they may be ignorant of Christ, and the Law of Nature? I instance in the millions of the *Abassine* Christians, who for above a thousand years never heard from the Pope or his emissaries.

Holden. l. 1. c. 9. p. 169. *Quæret an teneatur quispiam ad internum Divinæ fidei actum, quem nec semper fortasse in eius potestate situm novimus? Quamdiu sane arbitretur quispiam hujusmodi fidei actum lumini naturali & rationi oppositum & contrarium esse, nequaquam poterit ad illum eliciendum astringi.*

P. That cannot be denyed: For they have not the necessary means.

R. How then do you make your Churches proposal to be the necessary point to be *Explicitely believed of all*?

P. We do not mean it of all that will be saved: For

you

you hear that ſome may be ſaved without any explicite belief of Chriſt. But we mean it of all that *will* be in the Church, and be ſaved *there*.

R. But do you not hold and ſay, that out of the Church there is no ſalvation?

P. Some ſay ſo: and ſome ſay that It is *rare* out of the Church.

R. But are the *Ethiopian* Chriſtians out of the Church?

P. They are out of the true Church, being Schiſmaticks.

R. Why ſaid your Author before, that Infidels were not *formally* out of the Church who are invincibly ignorant?

P. But other Doctors are of another opinion.

R. But Chriſt is the Saviour of his body: Are not thoſe of the Church who are ſaved, or in a ſtate of ſalvation? What hold you of that?

P. Some ſay, They are all of the Church: and others that Chriſt ſaveth more than his Church: And ſome ſay, that They are of the Church Regenerate, but not of the Church Congregate. But few own this, becauſe it is your diſtinction: as of a viſible and inviſible Church.

R. *Qu*. III. But above all, I would know of you, what you mean by the *Catholick Church*, whoſe propoſal is neceſſary to the being of faith?

P. We mean the *Roman* Catholick Church: that is, the *Pope and his Subjects*.

R. Do you mean the Pope without a General Council, or a General Council without the Pope? or only both agreeing and conjunct?

R. You take advantage of our differences: but thoſe do but ſhew, that this is no point of faith. Some hold that the Pope alone may ſerve: and ſome, that the Pope in in a Provincial Council: and ſome that a General Council without him: But you heard *Veron* taketh in the Council, and it is no true Council without the Pope: And therefore the ſureſt opinion ſaith, that it muſt be both in Concord.

R. But what is the *Univerſal* Church whoſe Practice is made ſufficient inſtead of, or without a General Council?

P. It is the whole *Roman* Church real, diſtinct from the Repreſentative.

R. Is it the Clergy only, or the Laity only; or muſt it be both?

P. Both, but not equally; but in their ſeveral places.

R. Muſt it be *All* the Church, without any excepted? Or only the greater part?

P. Theſe are points not agreed of, and therefore not of faith. Some ſay that it muſt be ſo many as that the diſſenters be not conſiderable. But how many are conſiderable or inconſiderable is undetermined. Others ſay, It may be the minor part that practiſe, ſo be it the reſt do not contradict it, or do contrarily.

R. I will trouble you with no more ſuch queſtions, (though I have a multitude which ſhould be here reſolved) for I perceive that we muſt expect nothing but a Maze of uncertainties and confuſion.

We are next in order to *Agree* upon our *common principles* which muſt be *ſuppoſed* in our following Diſpute: For they that *Agree in nothing*, are uncapable of *diſputing* of *any thing*; ſeeing all concluſions of which we doubt, muſt be drawn from *more evident truths*, of which we are leſs doubtful, and reſolved into a conceded Principle.

 PART.

PART II.

The Principles which Papists and Protestants are agreed in: And therein the full Justification of all the Protestants Religion.

THe first common Principle: *That we are Men, having Reason, and Free-will, and Sense; whose Natural way of knowing things sensible, is by the perception of our senses, having no way of greater Certainty.*

R. I take it for a common principle, that we are *Men*, having *Reason*, and *Free-will*, and *Sense*: whose natural way of Knowing things sensible, is by the perception of our senses: And therefore that our rightly constituted or sound senses, with their due *media*, about their proper objects are to be trusted; being either certain, or we have no certainty.

P. I know what you intend: I grant it as you express it.

R. It must then be granted us, that there is *true Bread and Wine* in substance remaining after the words of the Mass-Priests consecration.

P. Yes: when you can prove, that the consecrated *Bread and Wine* are the proper objects of sense: which we deny; they being not now *Bread and Wine*.

R. Is it by the *Perception* of *sense* that you deny it? or by other means?

P. No:

P. No: It is by Faith and Reaſon which are above Senſe.

R. Now you come to *deny* the *Principle* which you *granted: Senſe* is the perceiver of its *own objects:* No *Faith*, no *Reaſon* can perceive them, but *by ſenſe*: And if *due ſenſation perceive* them, and Faith deny them, then *Faith* denyeth *ſenſe* to be the proper natural *perceiver of its objects*, and our judgement of things *ſenſible* to be ſuch as muſt follow that perception. But we muſt diſpute of this anon, and will not now anticipate it. Only remember, that if you deny *ſenſe* which is the firſt Principle, no mortal man is capable of diſputing with you, there being no lower principle to which we can have recourſe, and reſolve our differences.

The ſecond Principle: *That there is One only God, Infinite in Being, Power, Wiſdom and Goodneſs; Our Owner, Ruler and Chief Good; Moſt Holy, Juſt and True, and therefore cannot lye; but is abſolutely to be believed, and truſted, and loved.*

R. I need not repeat it: Do you not Agree with us in this?

P. Yes: Heathens (that are ſober) and Chriſtians are agreed in it.

R. You grant then, that this may be known by them that are no ſubjects of the Pope. Remember anon that we are not to be blamed for Believing God.

The third Principle: *That the whole frame of Nature within us and without us (within our reach) is the signal Revelation of God and his Will to man; called (Objectively) The Light and Law of Nature.*

R. I suppose that this also may pass for a common granted Principle.

P. Yes, as you express it: If we agree not of the Light and Law of Nature, we come short of Infidels, and meer Natural men.

R. Observe then, that we are Justified by your principles, for Believing and Trusting Gods *Natural Revelation.* The very first part of which is made to our senses: By *Natural Evidence* God sheweth us that Bread is Bread.

P. Yes: when sense is sound, and objects and *media* just, and God doth not contradict sense by supernatural Revelation.

The fourth Principle: *That Natural Revelation is before supernatural, and sense before faith, and we are Men (in order of Nature at least) before we are Christians, and the former is still presupposed to the later.*

R. This also I suppose is a granted Principle.

P. It is so: But see that you raise no false consequents from it.

R. I conclude from it, that He that denyeth the perception of sense to be the certain way of Judging of things

things ſenſible, denyeth all the Certainty of *faith*, and ſubverteth the very foundations of it: And that we are juſtified for our Aſſenting firſt to Gods Natural Revelations. It is God that made my *ſenſes and underſtanding*, and God that made the *object and media*, as *Bread and Wine*, and therefore *God deceiveth* me, if I be deceived in taking it for *Bread and Wine* after Conſecration. But God is to be *believed*, in his *firſt Revelations*.

P. You vainly call Senſation, and Intellection or Knowledge of things ſenſible by the name of *Believing*.

R. We will not vainly contend about the *Name*, if we agree of the *Thing*: But this leadeth me to another Principle.

The fifth Principle: *That the Knowledge of things fully ſenſible hath more quieting, ſatisfying Evidence, than our Belief of ſupernatural Revelations alone, as made to us by a Prophet or Apoſtle: And that where all the ſound ſenſes of all men living do agree about their near and proper ſenſible object, there is the moſt ſatisfying Evidence of all.*

R. I ſuppoſe that we are all agreed alſo in this principle.

P. As you *word* it we are: For our Divines diſtinguiſh of *Evidence and Certainty*: and are ſo far from ſaying that *Faith* hath more *Evidence* than *Senſe* and *Knowledge*, that it is ordinary with them to ſay, that this is the difference between *Faith* and *Knowledge*, and that *faith* hath not *Evidence*: but yet it hath no leſs certainty.

R. Some men uſe *words* firſt to ſport themſelves out of their underſtandings, and then to uſe others

to

to the same game. *Evidence* is nothing but the *Perceptibility* or *Cognoscibility* of a thing: by which we call it *Knowable*; which is the Immediate necessary qualification of an *Object* of *Knowledge*. *Certainty* is either *Objective*, which is nothing but this same *Cognoscibility* or *Evidence* as in a *satisfying* degree: Or it is *Subjective* or *Active*, which is nothing but the Infallible or *True*, and *quieting satisfactory knowledge* of a *Truth*. Where the *Certainty* of *Object* and *Act* concurr: For no man can be certain of a lye or untruth: For to be *Certain*, is to be certain that it is *True*: Those therefore would befool the world, who would perswade men, that a clear and confident perception of an untruth, or confident error, is *Certainty*. There may be Objective *Truth and Certainty* of the *Matter*, where there is not in us an Active or Subjective Certain Knowledge of it: But there can be no *Active Certainty* of an *Objective Uncertainty*, or *certain Knowledge* of a *lye*. Now if you mean that *faith* hath *Objective Certainty* without *Evidence* of *Certainty*, or Ascertaining *Evidence*, that is, but to *say* and *unsay*: It hath *Certainty* and no *Certainty*: For this *Certainty* and *Evidence* is all one. But if you mean that *Faith hath an Active Subjective Certainty* without an *Objective Certainty* in the Matter, you speak an impossibility and contradiction: as if you said, [*I clearly see a thing invisible or without light.*]

P. Do you think that our Divines knew not what they said, when they say that to believe without *Evidence* maketh *faith meritorious*?

R. The old asserters of this meant the same that Christ meant, when he saith to *Thomas* [*Blessed are they that have not seen*, and *yet have believed.*] There is a *sensible Evidence*, and an *Intelligible Evidence*. Faith hath not an *Immediate sensible Evidence*; that is, *we believe*

lieve things unseen, and above sense: And this is their meaning: We see not God, Christ, Heaven, Angels, *&c*. But *faith* hath alwaies *Intelligible Evidence* of *Verity*; and (as our Mr. *R. Hooker* saith) can go no further than it hath such Evidence.

However, I appeal to any that have not been disputed out of their wits, whether, If God would give us as full a *sight* of *Heaven* and Hell, and Angels and Blessed souls, as we have of the Bread and Wine before us, and as full a *Hearing* of all that they say, in justification of Holiness, or Lamentation of sin, and as full sensible acquaintance with the world we go to, and our title to it, as we have with this world, I say, whether this would not be more ascertaining and satisfactory to us, and banish all doubts, more than our present *faith* doth? I love not to hear men *lie as for God*, and talk and boast against *their experience*, as if the interest of faith required it. Things revealed to faith *Are Certain and Infallible*. But that is because we have *certain evidence* 1. That *God cannot lie*; 2. And that *God revealed them*; and so that they *are True*. But if we did *see, feel, taste*, &c. we should be *more certain*. Else why is it said, that we *now know but enigmatically* and as *in a glass*; and as *children*; but hereafter *shall see as face to face, and know as we are known, when faith is done away*, as being more Imperfect than *Intuition*. We have *evidence* to *prove*, that the Revelation made to *David, Isaiah, Jeremiah, Peter, Paul*, &c. were of God, and that their *words* are by us to be believed, *&c*. But to see, hear, taste, feel, *&c*. would be a more *quieting Assurance*.

Therefore when all *the sound senses of all men living*, perceive after consecration, that there is *Bread and Wine*, this *Certainty* is, 1. in order *antecedent to that of faith*, and 2. by *Evidence, more satisfying* and assuring than that of *meer faith*, as to a prophets Revelation; And therefore to reject it on pretence of *faith*, is a subversion of all natural methods of assurance; and is but pretended, I think, by your selves.

The sixth Principle. *That except those Immediate Inspirations which none but the Inspired do Immediately and clearly perceive, we have no Revelations from God, but by* signes; *which are* created beings; *and have their several* Natures, *and so may be called* Physical, *though signifying Moral things. And thus far our natural and supernatural Revelations agree.*

R. Every being is either *Uncreated* (which *is God only*) or Created (in a large sense, that is *Caused:*) What God Revealed to Christ, *Peter*, *Paul*, *&c.* we have knowledge of, but by *signes:* In *Scripture* these signes are *Words:* These *words* signifie partly the *mind of God*, and the speakers or writers, and partly the *matter spoken or written.* When it is said, that *It is impossible for God to lye*, it can mean nothing to us, but that it is impossible that God should make us a deceitful sign of his will. The voice of an Angel, Prophet, Apostle, a thousand Miracles, *&c.* are but *signes* of the *matter* and of Gods *will:* And if God can ordinarily make false *natural signes*, we are left unassured that he cannot make false signes by an Angel, or a Prophet, or a Miracle. And so all faith is left uncertain.

P. Then you will make God a lyar or deceiver whenever any man is deceived by natural signes.

R. Not so: For men may *deceive themselves* by taking those for *signes* of a thing which are *none*, and so by *misunderstanding* them. And the Devil and bad men nen may promote this deceit. But whenever God giveth man so *plain a sign* of the *Matter* and his *Will*, as that no errour of an *unsound sense*, an *unqualified object*, a *culpable* or diseased *fantasie* or *Intellect* interveneth, then if we are deceived it can be none but God that doth deceive us; which cannot be, because he *cannot lye*. And as it is an unresistible argument against the Dominican doctrine of *Physical Predetermination* as absolutely necessary *to all acts of natural or free agents*, that *If God physically predetermine every lyar to every lye, that is mentally conceived or uttered, then we have no certainty but he might do so by the Prophets and Apostles*; so is it as good an argument against *Papists*, that if he *ordinarily deceive the senses of all sound men* by a false appearance of things seeming *sensible*, he may do so also by the *audible* or *legible* words of a prophet.

The seventh Principle. *That he that will confute sense, and prove that we should not Judge according to its perceptions, must prove it by some more certain evidence that contradicteth it.*

R. I suppose you will not question this.

P. No: The *word* or Revelation of God is a more certain evidence.

R. How know you that there is any *word of God*, but by your senses?

P. But yet by *sense* I may get a *certainty* which is above that of things sensible. As I know by the world that there is a God, by a certainty above that of sense.

R. 1. If that were so, yet if things sensible be your *media*, you destroy your Conclusion by denying them, and undermine your own foundation.

2. But

2. But it is not true: The knowledge of the Conclusion can be no stronger than that of the principles, even of the weaker of them. If you are in any uncertainty whether there be Sun, Moon, Heaven, Earth, Man, Beast, Heat, Cold or any Created sensible being, you must needs be in as much doubt whether there be a God that made them.

The eighth Principle. *That* Believing *or* Assenting *is* Intellection of the Truth of something revealed, *and therefore must have Intelligible Evidence of Truth in the thing believed.*

R. I know that *Affiance* or *Trust* as it is the act of the *Will*, reposing it self quietly on the Believed fidelity of God, is not Intellection. But the *Assenting* act is an *Intellection* or an Act of *Knowledge* of a Verity; not as *Science* is narrowly confined to principles, but as *Knowledge* is taken *in genere* for *notitia*. So to believe is no other than to *know that this is true, because God saith it.* Joh.6.69. *We believe and are sure that thou art that Christ*, &c. Joh. 3. 2. *We know that thou art a Teacher come from God, for no man could do such works, &c.* Joh. 21. 24. *We know that his testimony is true* -- See Rom. 7. 14. & 8. 28. 2 Cor. 5. 1. *We know that if this earthly house*, &c. 1 Tim. 1. 8. 1 Joh. 3. 2. Joh. 8. 28, 32. 1 Cor. 15. 58. *We know that our Labour is not in vain, &c.* Therefore your denying the *certainty* where the *evidence* is most notorious, and telling men of *Meriting* if they will but believe your Church, without any *Evidence* of certainty, is a meer cheat.

The ninth Principle. *That Jesus Christ is the Son of God and the Saviour of the World, and that Christianity is the true Religion, and Gods appointed sufficient way to Heaven, including* Godliness, *which is its final part.*

R. By *Christianity* I mean both our *Believing, Loving and obeying Christ* as the way to the Father, and our Believing, Loving and Obeying God our Father, as the end of Christs Mediation : The *Knowledge of God* and the *Mediator* being *Eternal Life*, Joh. 17. 3. And as Taking a man for my Physicion, is taking him, by his *medicines to help me to my health*, and so *Health* is finally included, so taking Christ for my Saviour, is to take him *by faith* to be the means of bringing me to the *Love of God* and to Glory : And so I include *Godliness* in *Christianity*, and the Law of Nature in the Law of Grace.

P. We are agreed on the truth of this : but not of the *medium* by which it must be made known to us.

R. At the present I ask no more than that we agree in Christianity as the true and sufficient Religion and way to life.

The tenth Principle. *That Baptizing is our Christening : And that all that are truly Baptized are Christians, and members of the visible Church, untill they Apostatize or are justly excommunicate (at least.)*

P. I grant you all this as a common Principle with Christians.

R. Then you grant us, 1. That our Religion is the True Religion; of Gods appointment, sufficient to salvation: For it is *Christianity*, which you confessed to be such. 2. You grant that we are baptized into the true Catholick Church, which is the body of Christ.

The eleventh Principle. *That all that are truly Baptized have the pardon of all their sins, and have present right to salvation if they so die.*

R. I mean, that they that are *Internally true Consenters* to the *baptismal Covenant*, and are *baptized*, have all these benefits of Baptism: And that *Infants* have them as *rightly dedicated to God* and *baptized*: Do not you Consent to this?

P. Yes, you knew we do.

R. Then you fully grant, that all among the Protestants who in Infancy or at age are truly baptized are in a state of salvation: Why then would you make people believe that there is no salvation in our Churches, when you grant the right to all that are Baptized.

P. But you are not Baptized by lawful Ministers.

R. Take heed what you say: Your party holdeth that even Schismaticks and Hereticks Baptism is valid, if they have all that is essential to Baptizing in the doing of it: Yea that a lay mans, or womans baptizing is valid. If you deny it, I will shame you, by producing the common consent of your Doctors; and your censure

of

of *Cyprian*, and making the contrary doctrine to be a Heresie.

P. But you have not all that is essential to Baptism, because you are not intentionally Baptized, into the true Catholick Roman Church: For while you are not subject to the Pope, you are not baptized into the Church: and therefore *Bellarmine* sheweth that indirectly we are obliged to the Pope by baptism; which you intend not.

R. Come, come, strive not against your knowledge. 1. If our Baptism have not all that is essential, why do you never rebaptize Protestants when they turn to you? Do you not find that you condemn your selves? 2. Why do not you your selves put the name of the Pope into your words of baptism? 3. Doth your Tradition tell you that the ancient Churches did baptize men into a subjection to the Pope? 4. Did any of the Primitive Christians baptize men into the *name* or *subjection* of *Peter* or any Apostle? 5. Doth not *Paul* expresly renounce it as to himself and *Peter*, 1 Cor. 1. 12, 13, 14, 15. *Every one of you saith, I am of* Paul, *and I of* Apollo, *and I of* Cephas, *and I of Christ: Is Christ divided? Was* Paul *Crucified for you? or were ye baptized in the name of* Paul, &c. 6. Did not Christ himself tell us all that was Essential to baptism in his institution, *Matth.* 28 without making any mention of *Peter* or the Pope?

P. I cannot deny but our doctrine inferreth that all that are baptized among you have a true Sacrament, but not the Benefit of it, and so are not in a state of pardon and salvation: Or at least when you come to age, by refusing the Pope, you turn Hereticks and lose it.

R. I know some of your divided writers say that we have *Sacramentum*, but not *Rem Sacramenti*: But 1. You say that a Character is imprinted by Baptism, and all sin done away, and the person in a state of life, unless

less he come *feignedly* ; which you will not charge on Infants, nor can you prove it by those of the Anabaptists themselves that are baptized at age. And saith *Aquinas* when the fiction ceaseth, the fruits of baptism are obtained. 2. And it will be long ere you will prove that to be baptized into the name of the Trinity is uneffectual, if we leave out the Pope. 3. And you will hardly make a man understand what you mean by the validity of the Baptism of Hereticks and Schismaticks, if it neither take the Baptized into the true Visible Church, nor the invisible (or a state of saving grace).

And as to Infants losing it as you say at age by Heresie. 1. Will you save all the Anabaptists, that are baptized at age? If their baptism put them into a state of salvation, and they continue just of the same faith and mind that they were baptized in, sure that faith which put them in a state of salvation, will keep them in it ; or not be damning through defectiveness to morrow, which made them heirs of Heaven to day. But you cannot make your doctrines hang together. 2. And they that are Baptized in Infancy are baptized into the same faith which they continue in at age. The Minister intendeth no other : The Parents, Sponsors, *&c.* intend no other : And will that prove defective even to Salvation after, which was saving then? 3. If Baptism make us *Christians* ; and if *Christianity* be the *true Religion*, sufficient *in suo genere* to salvation, then we that continue in the *Christianity* which we were baptized into, by your confession continue in the true *saving Religion* ; And this is *all our Religion*.

P. It is not every one that owneth *Christianity* that shall be saved : Hereticks own it in general, and yet contradict it by their Heresies.

R. It is every *one* that *truly owneth Christianity* in *mind* and *will* that shall be saved : else Christianity were

were not a saving sufficient Religion : The question is not whether *objective Christianity* or *faith* be sufficient to save him that *believeth not*, or is not *subjectively* a Christian ; nor whether the *doctrine of faith* be sufficient in *omni genere* : But whether it be a *sufficient doctrine*, or *objective faith, in suo genere ?* If a *Heretick* deny any essential part of it, he *believeth not* that which he (really, understandingly and prevalently) *denyeth*. It is but the *Name* of *Christianity*, and not the *Thing*, which he owneth, who disowneth any of the *essence*. Our question is now whether our *professed objective Faith* be *true and sufficient ?* When you come to prove us *heretical* denyers of any of its essence, we will give you a sufficient answer.

The twelfth Principle. *That the Essenee of our Religion or Christianity as Active and Saving, is* Faith that worketh by Love : *Or such a Belief in God the Father, Son and Holy Ghost, as is accompanied with a true devoting of our selves to him, by Love and willingness to obey his Laws, so far as we know them ; in opposition to the temptations of the world, the flesh and the Devil : And he that is truly such shall be saved.*

P. I grant that he that truly Loveth God, shall be saved : But a Protestant cannot truly love God, because he hath not true faith.

R. Do you not agree and confess then, that If any Protestants do truly Love God, and are sincerely willing to obey his will, and to know it that they may obey it, such are of the true Religion and shall be saved, and that popery which denyeth their salvation is false ?

 P. If

P. If your falſe ſuppoſition were true, theſe falſe conſequents would be true: But you are all deceived when you think that you ſincerely Love God, and are willing to know and do his will.

R. 1. Let all Proteſtants note this firſt, that you grant that none but ☞ *falſhearted Hypocrites*, that are not what they profeſs to be, and *Love not God*, nor *would obey him*, ſhould *turn Papiſts*.

2. And if a man *cannot know his own Mind and Will*, what he *Loveth* and what he is *willing of*, no not about his *End* and *greateſt concernments*, how can he know when he *Believeth aright?* Why do you trouble the world thus with your noiſe about Believing the Propoſals of your Church, if a man *cannot know whether he believe or not?* ☞ And he that cannot *know* what he *Willeth, Chooſeth* or *Loveth*, can no more *know* what *he believeth*. For the *Acts* of the *Will* are more *plenary* and *eaſily perceived*. And do all *Papiſts know* their own *Hearts* or *Minds*, but no *Proteſtants?* What would you expect but indignation and deriſion by ſuch arguing as this, if you will go about the world and tell men, [*You none of you know your own Minds and wills, but we know them; You think you Love God, and are willing to obey him; but you are all miſtaken, it is not ſo with you: but you muſt believe our Pope and his Council, and then you may know your own minds and hearts.*] They that believe you on theſe rates, deſerve the deceit of believing you; and puniſh themſelves.

The thirteenth Principle. *That when Christ described all the Essence of Christianity, by our Believing in and being baptized into, the name of the Father, the Son and the Holy Ghost, the Apostles and first Pastors of the Churches, instructed people to understand the meaning of these three Articles; And the ancient Creed called the Apostles, is the exposition of them, as to Belief: And that this Creed was of old the symbol of the true faith, by which men were supposed sufficiently qualified for baptism, and distinguished from Hereticks: which after was enlarged by occasion of heresies to the Nicene and Constantinopolitane Creed; To which that call d* Athanasius's *was added as a fuller explication of the doctrine of the Trinity: And he that believed all these, was taken for one of the true Christian Religion, which was sufficient* in suo genere *to salvation.*

P. All that was *then Necessary* to be explicitely believed, *necessitate medii*, was expressed in the Creeds (if not more): But not all that is *now necessary* when the Church hath proposed more.

R. 1. Some of you say, no more is necessary *ut medium*, but to believe that *God is*, and that *he is a rewarder of them that diligently seek him*: Others say that the chief articles of the Creed also are commonly necessary: And in your discord we lay no great weight on your Opinions. 2. But is not *Christianity* the same *Thing now* as it was at the *beginning*? Is *Baptism altered*? Hath not a *Christian* now the same *definition* as *then*? Are not *Christs promises* and the *Conditions* the same? Shall not he that was a *Christian* then, be ſaved if he were *now alive?* May not we be *Chriſtians*, and *ſaved* by the ſame *Conſtitutive Cauſes* which made men *Chriſtians*, and *ſaved* them in the *primitive Churches?* Subvert not Chriſtianity, and confound not the Church, and cheat not poor ſouls, by labouring to hide the *eſſence* of *Chriſtianity*, and ſuch plain important truths. You cannot deny our faith to be *true*, without condemning the ancient Church and Chriſtianity it ſelf: While we aloud profeſs that the *Chriſtian faith explained in all the ancient Creeds*, is the faith which we own, in its Eſſentials explicated.

The fourteenth Principle. *That the Books which the Proteſtants commonly receive as Canonical Scriptures, are in the agreeing Original Copies, as to the very words, and in true Tranſlations as to the ſence, the moſt true Infallible word of God.*

R. I grant that where the *Copies diſagree* by various Readings, we are no more ſure that any of them is the word of God, than we are ſure, that ſuch a Copy is righter than all that differ from it. But as long as the *eſſence of Chriſtianity* on which our *Salvation* is laid, is in the *Covenant of Grace*, explained *in Credendis* in the *Creed*, and *in Petendis*, in the *Lords Prayer*, and *in Agendis*, in the *Decalogue* as explained by *Chriſt*. And no one Duty or material doctrine of our Religion dependeth on the *various Lections*, but thoſe texts that *Agree* are ſufficient to eſtabliſh them all; yea, as *Franc. à Sancta Clara ſyſtem. fid.* profeſſeth, the ordinary *Tranſlations* ſo agree, as that no *material point* of *Religion* doth depend on any of *their differences*; It is as much as we aſſert, that the *Agreeing Original Copies*, and

and the *ſound Tranſlations*, ſo far as they are ſuch, are the True Infallible word of God; the *former* both as to *words and ſence*, and the *later* as to *ſence alone*. Do you not grant this?

P. We grant the Scripture as you ſay to be Gods Infallible word; But 1. You cannot *know it to be ſo*, becauſe you take it not on the Roman Churches Authoritative Propoſal; 2. And you leave out part of it.

R. 1. Whether we can *know it*, ſhall be tryed in due place. 2. And whether we have *All of it*, or *enough*, is another queſtion, to be debated when you will. You grant us expreſly that which we now deſire; which is the *Infallible Truth* of our *Canonical Scripture*. And this is *All our Religion*, containing not only the *Eſſentials*, but all *the Integrals*, and *Accidentals* needful to be recorded. So that *All the Proteſtants Religion is confeſſed to be Infallibly True*.

And from hence further note, that in all our diſputes, you are obliged to *be the defendants*, as to *Truth*: For we deny the *Truth* of much of your Religion, but you deny not the *Truth* of one word of ours: but only the *Plenitude* or *Sufficiency*.

P. The name of a Proteſtant was never known till *Luthers* time: And the occaſion of it was a particular Proteſtation of the *German* Princes, and not directly a *Proteſting* againſt *Popery*.

R. It is not *Names* but *Religion* which we diſpute of. And it is that which each party *Profeſſeth* to be *their Religion*. Therefore you muſt take *our Profeſſion* or you change the *ſubject* of the diſpute. And we *profeſs*, that the *Law of Nature* (which no ſober man queſtioneth) and the *Scriptures*, are *All our Religion*. Therefore if you pleaſe you ſhall ſuppoſe that the name *Proteſtant* were not now in the world: It doth not ſignifie our Religion. But *we now* uſe it to ſignifie our *Proteſt-*

ing against Popery, or that we agree *in substance*, and in *rejecting Popery*, with those that made that particular *Protestation* mentioned by you.

Names are oft given from *accidents* ; as *Africanus*, *Germanicus*, *Britannicus*, &c. to several Roman Captains ; when yet their *Humanity* was the same before they were so named.

P. Turks, Socinians, Quakers, *&c.* Protest against Popery : It seems then they are *Protestants* too ; and your companions.

R. 1. Thus some men study to deceive, by turning from the question to another. Our question I tell you is *Whether* the *Religion of the Protestants* be *Infallible ?* and not, *Whence is their name ?* 2. But by a *Protestant* we mean only one that taketh the *Scripture for the Rule*, and *Christianity* for the *Essence* of his Religion : Which no one doth that denyeth any *essential* part of it. If we do so, prove it, and you shall have our answer. How do you judge of any man among your selves that taketh Gods word proposed by your Church for his Religion, and yet mistaketh the Church in any point : As *Durandus* that thought the matter of Bread continues, whom *Bellarmine* yet denyeth to be an Heretick. So is it with any among us that mistake the sence of Scripture in some such point.

When a Name is put upon any person or party from a common accident, you may if you will call all by that name which that accident agreeth to : And so *Papists* are called by some *Non-conformists* now in *England*, because they Conform not : But the world knoweth well enough that it is *Protestants* which are commonly meant by that name, and not Papists, Quakers, Seekers, *&c.* though [they] *conform not*. And so you may say if it please [you]r self that Turks, Jews, Heathens, Socinians, Qua[ker]s, Ranters, are *Protestants*, because they *Protest against*,

against, or reject Popery: But the world knoweth who is meant by the Name, Even *Christians rejecting proper Popery.*

And for my part, I deal openly with you, I care not if the name *Protestant* were utterly cast aside; It any man be so deceived by it as 1. Either to think that it signifieth the *Essence* of our Religion (unless you mean as we *Protest* for Christianity.) 2. Or that we take those called *Protestants* for the *whole Catholick Church*, they make it an occasion of their own deceit: Names of distinction are used, because men know not else readily how to speak intelligibly of one another without circumlocutions: And then cometh the Sectarian, and taketh his *Party*, for *all the Church* (at least which he may lawfully Communicate with), and the *name* of his party to notifie *his Religion.* And then comes the *crafty Papist*, and pretends from hence that such a *named Religion* is new; and asketh you, *where was there any* (e.g.) *Protestants before* Luther?

My Religion is *naked Christianity*, the same as is where the name of a *Protestant* is *not known*, and as was *before it was known*; and as if the name of the *Pope* had never been known. But now the *Pope* and his *Monarchical Usurpation* over all the world, *are risen* and *known*, I am one of those that protest against them, as being against Christianity which is my Religion; But so as to addict my self to the opinions of no man or party that opposeth them, wholly and absolutely and beyond evidence of truth: I take the *Reformed Churches*, to be the *soundest* in the world: But I take their Confessions to be all the Imperfect expressions of men; and the Writings of Protestant Divines to be some more clear and sound; and some more dark, empty, and less sound, and in many things I differ from many of them. Choose now whether you will call me a *Protestant* or not; I tell

tell you *my Religion*, which is *simple Christianity*: Names are at your own Will. I could almost wish that there were no name known besides that of CHRISTIAN as notifying our *faith* and *Religion*, in the Christian world (Though as notifying *Heresie* and *sin*, there must be proper names, as in *Rev.* the name *Nicolaitans* is used). Even the word *Catholick* had long a narrower sense in the Empire with many than I now own it in. Though as it signifieth *One that is of the Church Universal*, loveth *Universally* all *true Christians*, and hath Communion with them in Faith, Love, and Hope; so I like it, and am A CATHOLICK CHRISTIAN. I dispute for nothing else; I perswade this person here in Doubt, to nothing else; but 1. To hold fast to true and meer Christianity; 2. To *Reject* all in Popery or any other Sect that is *Evidently against it*; 3. To *suspend* his belief of all *thats doubtful*, and to receive nothing as a part of *Divine faith* or *Religion*, till he *be sure* that indeed it is of God.

And now these Principles being supposed, let us proceed, and try whether Popery be of God or not.

PART.

PART III.

The Protestants Reasons against Popery.

D. I Have heard what you have said in stating the *Protestants Religion:* I now expect to hear *what Reasons you have against that which you call Popery:* And afterwards that you *prove* all that you charge upon it. But I adjure you first that you say nothing but what you believe in your conscience to be the truth, as one that looketh to be judged for it.

R. With many Papists confident and vehement protestations go instead of Arguments, and we oft hear them say, [*If this be not true, I am content to be torn in a thousand pieces: We will seal it with our blood: We will lay our salvation on it: And do you think we have not souls to save? &c.*] Which is much like as if they would end all Controversies by *laying Wagers* that they are in the right, or by *protesting* that they are *honester and credibler men* than their adversaries: And it is no more than a Quaker or other such Sectary will say: the most proud and ignorant being usually the most confident: But yet though I expect not that you should receive any thing from me, upon *Protestations,* but upon *Proofs,* I will here promise you that I will charge nothing on the Papists, but what in my Conscience I am verily perswaded to be true.

The Reaſons which reſolve me againſt *Popery* are theſe and ſuch like.

I. *Reaſon*, Their Doctrine of *Tranſubſtantiation* is ſo *notoriouſly falſe* and *inhumane*, even contrary to the fulleſt aſcertaining evidence that mankind can expect on earth, (*viz.* for all men on pain of damnation to believe, that there is *no Bread*, and *no Wine*, when all the ſoundeſt ſenſes of any men in the world, do perceive Bread and Wine, by *ſeeing* it, *taſting* it, *feeling* it, *ſmelling* it, and by the *notorious effects*; and all this built upon *no Revelation of God*, *no Reaſon* at all, nor any true *conſent* of the *Primitive Church*, but *clean contrary to them all*;) that I ſolemnly profeſs, that I find it an *utter Impoſſibility* to believe it: And it often puts me to a doubt, Whether it be poſſible for any mortal man unfeignedly and fully to believe it, and Whether there be *really any ſuch Papiſt in the world*: or Whether moſt do not for carnal reſpects take on them to believe it, when they do not; or rather the Vulgar underſtand their words, as not really excluding the true being of *Bread and Wine*; and the reſt only ſomewhat overawing their own reaſon with a reverence of their Church, ſo far as not to *contradict*, or ſo far as *notionally* to own it, when they do not from the heart believe the thing.

So many contradictions, abſurdities, and impieties are to be by them believed with it, that I am ſure no man that underſtandeth them, can poſſibly believe them all.

And all this muſt be done by *Miracles*, *ſtupendious miracles*, *daily* or *common miracles*, which *every Prieſt* can do at *his pleaſure*, and *never fail*, *ſober* or *drunken*, greater than raiſing a man from the dead; ſo that

that every beastly, sordid, ignorant Priest, shall do more miracles by far, than ever Jesus Christ did in all his life on earth, as far as we know by the holy Records, (if he live as long). He that can believe all this, may next believe, that there is neither Earth under his feet, nor the Firmament over his head, nor Water, nor Air, nor any other Creature, and that he hath no *being* himself.

II. *Reason:* The Faith or Religion of the Papists, as described by themselves, is so far from Infallibility, as that it is utterly uncertain, unintelligible, and meer contradiction and confusion; and a changeable thing; so that no man knoweth whether he have it or not, and whether he have it all; But whoever hath it, he hath certainly a hodge-podge of truth and falshood.

III. *Reason.* Their Papacy, which essentiateth their Church, is a horrid Usurpation of Christs own Prerogative, and of an Office to do that which is incomparably above the Natural Power or Capacity of any mortal man; even to be the Apostle and Governour of the whole world (of Christians at least); To take Charge of all the souls on earth; to teach and call those that are uncalled, and to Rule those that are baptized: even at the Antipodes, and in all those unknown or inaccessible parts of the world, which he hath no knowledge of: A far more arrogant undertaking, than to be the Civil Monarch of all the earth; and utterly impossible for him to perform, and which never was performed by him.

IV. *Reason.* The said Papacy is an arrogant Usurpation of the Power of all the Christian Princes and Pastors upon earth, or of a Power over them, never given by Christ: It setteth up a Kingdom in a Kingdom, and taketh from Pastors the power which Christ gave them, over their particular flocks.

V. *Reason.* The said Papacy is a meer humane Institution: They confess themselves, that it is not of Divine faith that the Bishop of *Rome* is St. *Peters* Successor by Divine Right: It is no article of their *own faith*: But History fully assureth us, that it was but in the *Roman* Empire, that the *Roman* Bishop was made Supream: as the Archbishop of *Canterbury* is in *England*: And that he standeth on the same *humane* foundation as the *other four Patriarchs* of the Empire did. And that their *General Councils* were called by the *Emperours*, and were called *General* only with respect to that Empire. And there never was such a thing as a *General Council* of *all* the *Christian world*, nor ever can be: And that there never was such, is most notorious yet by the Names subscribed to all the Councils. But they abuse the world, and claim that power *over all the Christians on earth*, which *one Prince* gave his subject-Prelates *in his Empire*: As if the *General Assembly* of *Scotland* or *France* should pretend to be a *General Council* of *the world*, and the Archbishop of *Canterbury* should call himself Archbishop of all the Church on earth, and claim the government of it.

VI. *Reason:* The said Papacy hold their claim of *Supream Government* as by *Gods appointment* (though they confess as before said, that it is not *de fide*, that the Pope succeedeth *Peter* by Divine right) and this notoriously *Contrary to the Judgement and Tradition of the far greatest part of the Churches in the world:* General Councils (such as they had) and the sense of the greatest part of Christians have determined against the Papal claime. And *Tradition* condemneth them to this day, while they plead Tradition.

VII. *Reason:* It is Treason against Christ for the Papists who are but a *Sect*, and not the third part of the Christians in the world, to call themselves the *whole Church*, and unchurch all the rest, and seek to rob Christ of the far greatest part of his Kingdom, by denying them to be such: As if they would deny two third parts of this Kingdom to be the Kings. They are Sectaries and Schismaticks by this arrogant dividing from all the rest, and appropriating the name and priviledges of the Church to themselves alone.

VIII. *Reason:* By making an *unlawful* and *Impossible Condition* and Center of *Church Union*, they are the *greatest Schismaticks* in all the world: The greatest *Dividers* of the Church upon pretence of *Unity:* As he would be a divider of this Kingdom, who would set up a *Vice-King* without the Kings authority, and say that none that subject not themselves to him, shall be taken for subjects of the King.

IX. *Reason:* They studiously brand themselves with Satans mark of malice, or uncharitableness and cruelty to mens souls: while they sentence to *damnation two third parts* of the Christian world, because they will not be the subjects of their Pope: And they think their way to Heaven is safest, because they are bolder than us in damning other Christians: Whereas *Love* is the mark by which Christs Disciples must be known to all.

X. *Reason:* They are inhumanely *cruel to mens bodies:* And this is their very Religion: For the Council at the *Laterane* under *Innocent* the third decreed, that those that believe not, or deny Transubstantiation are Hereticks, and all Temporal Lords shall exterminate them from their Dominions: That is, no man shall be suffered to live under any Christian Lord, that will not renounce all his senses, and profess that he believeth that they are all deceived by God himself; which is not only to renounce their *Humanity*, but their *Animality* or sense it self. So that *no men indeed*, are to be suffered to live, but only such as *deny themselves to be men:* What Heathens, what Turks, did ever exercise such Inhumane fury? Besides their burning and tormenting men as Hereticks that will not do all this and more, and will not say as they require them.

XI. *Reason:* Their Church *indeed* is *invisible*, while they deny it, and an unknown thing: For, 1. Men are forced into it by such bloody Laws, as that they cannot rationally be known to be *Consenters:* 2. And of them say, That they *that believe not in Christ*, have *saving faith*, and *are in the Church*, if they had not sufficient means.

XII. *Reason:* The Papacy doth intolerably tyrannize over Kings, and teach such Doctrines of Perjury and Rebellion, as their very Religion; as is not in the practice of it to be endured in any Kingdom; nor dare they fully practise it: The Crowns and Lives of Princes being at the mercy of the Pope; As the said *Laterane* Council sheweth.

XIII. *Reason:* Their *Church* is oft *Essentially unholy*, *heretical and wicked*, because the *Pope* is often so, who is an *Essential part* of it: And therefore it is not the *holy Catholick Church*. General Councils have upon examination judged their Popes to be *Hereticks*, *Schismaticks*, *Adulterers*, *Murderers*, *Simonists*, yea, guilty of *Blasphemy* or *Infidelity* it self. And the *Church* cannot be *Holy*, whose *Essential part* is so unholy.

XIV. *Reason:* Their Churches *succession* is so notoriously *interrupted*, and their Papacy so often altered in its causes, as that it is become a confounded and a meer *uncertain* thing. So many notorious or judged

Hereticks, Simonists, Murderers, Sodomites, Adulterers have possessed the Seat, who were therefore *uncapable*, that the line of succession must needs be interrupted by them. And so many wayes have they been made or elected, sometimes by the people, sometimes by the City-Presbyters, sometimes by Emperours, sometimes by Cardinals, sometimes by Councils, that if any *one way* of *Election* be necessary, they have lost their Papacy long ago. If *no one* way be necessary, then the Turk may make a Pope.

XV. *Reason*: Their Church called *One*, is really *two in specie*; *one* Headed by a *Pope*, and *another* by a *General Council*: For while the *Head* or *Supream Ruler* is an *Essential part*, and *one part* of the people own *one Head* and another part own *another Head*, (as they do) the Churches thus constituted cannot be *One*.

And also *de individuo* there have been long two or three Popes at once, and consequently two or three Churches: And to this day none knoweth which was the right.

XVI. *Reason*: They plead for a Church which never had a being in the world; that is, *All Christians Headed by one Pope*; When *all the Christian world* did never take him for their Head, nor were governed by him to this day.

XVII. *Reason*: They dreadfully injure the *holy Scriptures*, as if *Jesus Christ*, and all the *Prophets* and *Apostles* in all those Sacred Records, had not had *skill*

or

or *will* to ſpeak *intelligibly*, and *plainly* to deliver us the doctrines neceſſary to ſalvation : But they make their *Voluminous Councils* more *intelligible* and *ſufficient*; as if they had done better than Chriſt and his Apoſtles : And when men muſt only *Diſcern Gods Laws*, and *Judge Cauſes by the Law*, they make themſelves *Judges of the Law it ſelf*, that is, of God the Judge of all, and of that Law by which they muſt be judged.

XVIII. *Reaſon :* There is no other Sect of Chriſtians under Heaven which hath ſo many differences among themſelves, or have written ſo many Books againſt one another as the Papiſts : And though many of them are of great importance, yea, ſome are about the very Eſſence or Conſtitutive Head of their Church, yet have they no handſomer way to palliate all by, than by ſaying that theſe are but *Opinions*, and no *Articles of faith*, and the Infallible Judge *dare* not decide them : No though it be diverſity of *Expoſitions* of *Gods own Word*, yet Commentators ſtill differ without any hope of a deciſion, as if *Gods Word* were not to be *believed*, but were only the matter of *uncertain Opinion*, till the Pope and Council have expounded it, and no more Scripture is *de fide* than they expound.

XIX. *Reaſon :* Perjury is made the very Character of their Church, or the brand by which it is ſtigmatized; As is viſible 1. In the *Trent Oath* impoſed on their Clergy, which whoever taketh he is immediately perjured : and 2. By their diſobliging men from Oaths and Vows ; even the Subjects of Princes from their *Oaths of Allegiance*, whenever the Pope ſhall excom-

 municate

municate them, and give their Dominions to others, as is decreed *Concil. Later. sub Innoc.* 3. *Can.* 3.

XX. *Reason*: They are guilty of *Idolatry* in their ordinary Worship by the Mass: while they worship *Bread* as their *Lord God*: Nor will it justifie them to say, that if they *thought* it to be *Bread*, they would not worship it: Any more than it would justifie *Julian* to say, that he would not worship the *Sun*, if he thought not that it was *God*: And they confess, that if it prove to be still *Bread*, their Worship will prove *Idolatry*: and we desire no other proof.

And I am not able to justifie their sending God his Worship by a Cross, Crucifix, or other *Image*, as a *medium cultum*, from being a gross Violation of the second Commandment: (which they leave out).

XXI. *Reason*: Their Religion greatly tendeth to *Mortifie Christianity*, and turn it into a *dead Image*, by destroying much of its life and power: 1, By *befriending Ignorance*, and hiding the *holy Scripture*, forbidding all the people to *read them in a known tongue* without a special license: blaspheming Gods Word, as if so read, it had more tendency or likelihood to *hurt* men than to *profit* them, to *damn* them than to *save* them; when they will say otherwise of all their own Vulgar postils and such like writings.

2, And by teaching the people a *blind devotion*, *viz.* to *pray* in an *unknown tongue*, and to worship God by *words not understood*.

3. And by making up a Religion much, if not *far most*, of *external formalities*, and a multitude of *ceremonies*, and the *opus operatum* of their various Sacra-

ments; As if God delighted in ſuch actions as befit not the acceptance of a grave and ſober man; or as if *Guilt* and *Sin* would be wiped off, and charmed away into virtue and holineſs, by ſuch corporeal motions, ſhews and words.

XXII. *Reaſon:* Their Religion, though it thus tend to *gratifie the ungodly* by deceitful remedies and hopes, yet is very *uncomfortable* to the godly. For, 1. By it no man can know that he is a *true believer*, and not a child of Hell, (much leſs that he ſhall be ſaved:) For they teach that no Divine can tell them what Articles are neceſſary to be believed to ſalvation: But they muſt be ſo many as are ſuited to every *ones capacity*, and *means*, during his life. And no man living can know that he underſtandeth and believeth *as much* as his capacity and means were in their kind ſufficient to: Nay, there is no man that hath not been culpably ignorant of ſomewhat which he might have known.

2. Mens Sacramental receptions and comforts depend on the *Intention* of the *Prieſt*, which no man knoweth.

3. Almoſt all Godly men muſt expect the *fire of Purgatory:* and conſequently none of them *can be rationally willing to dye:* Becauſe *this life* is better than *Purgatory*; and no man will deſire to go from hence into the fire: And ſo by making *all men unwilling to dye*, it deſtroyeth a *heavenly mind*, and killeth *faith*, and *hope*, and *love*, and *holy joy*, and tempteth men to be *worldlings*, and to love this life better than the next. Yea, it tempteth men to be afraid of Martyrdom, leſt (dying in Venial ſins, as all do) they go to a Purgatory fire, more terrible than Martyrdom.

XXIII. *Reason:* Their Doctrine is not only contrary to many express Texts of Holy Scripture, but also contrary to it self: One Pope and one Council having decreed one thing, and another the clean contrary.

XXIV. *Reason:* All this evil is made more pernicious, by that professed Impenitence which is included in the conceit of their Churches Infallibility: For they that hold themselves Infallible, do profess never to Repent, of any thing in which they suppose themselves to be so. And as Repentance is the great evidence of the pardon of sin; so *Impenitency* is that mortal sign of an unpardoned soul, without which no sin doth qualifie the sinner to be Excommunicated by man, or damned by God: And a sin *materially less, is more Mortal unrepented* of, than a greater truly lamented and forsaken.

XXV. *Reason:* Every honest godly Protestant may be as sure that Popery is false, as he is that he is himself sincere, and Loveth God, and is truly willing to obey him. And no man can turn Papist, without self-contradiction, who is a true Christian, and an honest man: For by turning Papist he confesseth himself to be before a false-hearted hypocrite, who neither Loved God, nor sincerely desired to obey him, nor was true to his Baptismal Covenant. For it is a part of Popery to believe that none are in a state of salvation, but the *Subjects of the Pope*, or members of the Papal Church: And consequently that no others have true Faith, Repentance

pentance or Love to God: Or elſe that God is falſe in promiſing ſalvation, to all that have true Faith, Repentance and Love to God. All therefore that know their own hearts to be truly devoted to God, are ſafe from Popery; And ſeeing it is agreed on both ſides, that none can or ought to turn Papiſts but *ungodly hypocrites* (or Knaves) no wonder if ſuch are deluded by the moſt palpable deceits, and forſaken of God whom they perfidiouſly forſook.

I will name you no more: If I make theſe, or any one of theſe good (as I undertake to prove them all), you will ſee that I refuſe not my ſelf to be a Papiſt without ſufficient cauſe.

And yet by this charge you will ſee that I am none of their extream adverſaries: I paſs by abundance of Doctrinal differences, wherein by many they are moſt deeply charged: Not as *Juſtifying them* againſt all or moſt ſo charged on them, but 1. As giving you thoſe Reaſons which moſt *move my ſelf*, and which I am moſt able to make good, and leaving every one to his proper work: 2. And as one that have *certainly found out*, that in *many doctrinals* ſeeming to be the matter of our wideſt difference, we are thought by many to differ much more than we do; 1. The difference lying moſt in *Words*, and *Logical Notions*, and various wayes of mens expreſſing their conceptions: 2. And the animoſity of men engaged in *Parties* and *Intereſts* againſt each other, cauſing moſt to take all in the worſt ſenſe, and to make each other ſeem far more erroneous than they are, and to turn *differing names* into *damnable hereſies*: And 3. Few men having *Will* and *Skill* to ſtate controverſies aright, and cut off miſtaken ſeeming differences: 4. And few having *honeſty* and *ſelf-denyal*

enough

enough to incurr the cenſure of the ignorant Zealots of their own party, by ſeeming but impartial and juſt to their adverſaries.

I mean in ſuch points, as 1. The Nature of Divine faith, Whether it be a perſwaſion that I am pardoned, *&c.* 2. Of Certainty of ſalvation, 3. And Certainty of perſeverance, 4. Of Sanctification, 5. Of Juſtification, 6. Of Good works, 7. Of Merit, 8. Of Predeſtination, 9. Of Providence and the Cauſe of Sin: 10. Of Free-will, 11. Of Grace, 12. Of Imputation of Righteouſneſs, 13. Of Univerſal Redemption, 14. Of Original Sin, and divers others: In all which I cannot juſtifie them, but am ſure that the difference is made commonly to ſeem to be that which indeed it is not: In the true impartial ſtating whereof *Lud. Le Blanck* hath begun to do the Chriſtian Churches moſt excellent ſervice, worthy our great thanks, and his bearing all the Cenſures of the ignorant.

PART

PART IV.

The First Charge made good against Transubstantiation: In which Popery is proved to be the Shame of Humane Nature, Contrary to SENSE, REASON, SCRIPTURE and TRADITION, or the judgement of the Antient and Present Church; devised by Satan to expose Christianity to the Scorn of Infidels.

CHAP. I.

The First Reason to prove Transubstantiation false.

R. THe Papists Belief of Transubstantiation is, that There is a change made of *the whole substance of the Bread into the body of Christ*, and *of the whole substance of Wine into his blood.* Their opinion (called their faith) hath two parts: The first is, that *There is no more true Proper Bread and Wine after the words of Consecration, Hoc est Corpus meum.* The second is, that *There is the true proper Flesh and Blood of* Jesus Christ, *under the species* (as they call them) *of Bread and Wine.*

It

It is the first that I shall now prove false: And you must not forget the state of the Question, which is not, *Whether Christs Body and Blood be present?* But *Whether there remain any Bread and Wine?*

Aquin. p. 3. q. 75. a. 5. ad 3. *Fides non est contra sensum, sed est de eo ad quod sensus non attingit.* But doth not sense say, Here is Bread and Wine?

Arg. I. If there remain *no Bread and Wine* after the Consecration, then all the senses of all the sound men in the world are deceived, or all mens perception of these sensible things deceived, though there be due magnitude, site, distance of the object, a due abode, and a due *medium* and no depravation of the sense or intellect. But this Consequent is notoriously false, (as shall be proved) Therefore Popery is false.

1. That *all mens senses* perceive *Bread and Wine*, or *all mens Intellects by their senses*, will not be denyed. Not only *Protestants*, but *Greeks*, *Mahometans*, *Heathens*, *Papists*, all persons perception by sense is here the same: Therefore it is *sound senses* or else there are *none sound* in the world.

2. It is not *one sense*, but *all*. The *eye seeth* Bread and Wine: The *hand* and *mouth feel it*; The *palate tasteth* it; The *smelling sense smelleth* the Wine; yea, and the *ear heareth* it poured out.

3. It is *in due quantity*, and not an undiscernable *Atome*.

4. It is *near the sense*, and neither by too much distance or nearness made insensible.

5. It hath a *due abode*, and is not made insensible by *hasty passing by*.

6. The *air*, and *light*, and all *necessary media* of perception are present. So that there is nothing wanting to the *sensibility* of the object.

P. And

P. And how do you prove all or any of these? For ought you know, the *media* may be *undue*, the magnitude, site, distance, abode, may not be what they seem to be; and so you prove not what you say.

R. All that I am now saying, is, that *All men of sound sense, in the world have these immediate clear perceptions*: The *Intellect by sense* perceiveth the object as *quantitative*, as *near*, &c. This you dare not deny: So that if this perception be false, and here be no Bread and Wine, then *Sense* or the *Intellect* discerning by the means of sense, is deceived.

P. I say that the *Senses* or *Intellects perception* are deceived.

R. I prove that they are not deceived; or at least, that this *kind of perception* is the *most certain* that man on earth is capable of, and is to be *trusted* to by *all men*, and disbelieved or contradicted by none.

Reason I. Because that *humane nature* is so formed, that the *Intellect* hath no other way of *perceiving things sensible*, but as they are first perceived by the *sense*, and by it transmitted to the *Intellect* (or made its objects): And if about *Spirits* it hold not, that *There is nothing in the Intellect, which was not first in the sense*: yet about *things sensible*, it doth undenyably hold: And also that the *Intellect of it self* is not *free* to perceive things sensible otherwise than as they are *sensed*, or not to perceive them; but is *naturally necessitated* to perceive them. So that it is a contradiction for a man to be a man, consisting of a *reasonable soul*, with *sensitive faculties* and a body, and yet not to be formed to judge of *things sensible* as *sense perceiveth them*.

P. Then mad men cease to be men, if they judge otherwise.

R. Mad men are your fittest presidents: But, 1. I told you how mans nature is made by God to judge of

things:

things: I told you not that this nature may not be *vitiated*, and *hindered* from right action. Did I ever say, that the *eye* may not be *blinded*, or the understanding distracted? Blind men and mad men judge not according to the tendency of *Nature*, and therefore *misjudge*. The Connexion of the Intellect to the sense is essential to man as man; but so is not the *soundness* or right exercise of his faculties.

Reason II. Hence I argue, that *sensation* and the *understandings perception thereby*, is the *first perception* of mans soul, and all that *follow* are but the *rational improvements of it*, and therefore ever *presuppose* it: The natural order of the souls apprehensions is this, beyond all controversie. First *Sense* perceiveth *things sensible*, and the *Imagination* the *Images* of them. Next the *Understanding* by a *simple perception* conceiveth of them as it findeth them in the *imagination*. Thirdly, then by this *Thinking* or *Knowing*, we perceive also our *own Act*, that we do so *Think* or *Know*. And then Fourthly, We *compound* our *conceptions*, and form *organical notions*, and spin out *conclusions* from what we first perceive. Now if the *first perceptions* be *uncertain* or *false*, it must needs follow, that all those *following thoughts*, and *reasonings* which do but *improve* them, are at least *as uncertain* and *false*, if not more. So that there can be no more certainty in any of the *Conclusions* as such, than there is in the *premises* and *principles*. Therefore if mans *first* and *most natural necessary* perceptions are *false*, all the following actions or reasonings of his mind must be no better. All being finally resolved into these *perceptions by sense*, there is no Truth or Certainty in mans mind at all, if there be none in these.

Reason III.

Reason III. Else you would infer, that *God is not at all to be Believed*, and that there is no such thing as *Divine Faith and Religion in Certainty* in the world: And so you would bring in, by unavoidable consequence, far worse *Impiety*, and *Irreligiousness* than *Mahomet* or *Julian*, or any Idolaters that I hear of on the earth. For you directly will overthrow the *Divine Veracity*, or *Truth* of *Gods Revelations*, which is the *Formal Object of Faith*, without which, it is *no Faith*.

P. A heavy charge, if you can make it good.

R. To make it good, do but first observe, 1. That *Gods Essential Will* or *mind* is not *in it self* immediately seen by man; but known only by some *Revelation*.

2. That this Revelation is nothing but some SIGNES: For there is nothing in the Universe of Beings, but GOD and CREATURES and the ACTS or Works of Creatures. Now it is not *Gods own Essence* which is the *Revelation* in question. Therefore it must be either *A Creature* (or work of God), or an *Act* or *Work* of a *Creature*. As the *voice* on *Mount Sinai*, and that of Christ at his baptism and transfiguration, and the written Tables of Stone, &c. were either the *works* of God immediately, and so created *Signs* of his mind; or else the *Acts* of *Angels*, and so *Imperate Signs* of his mind. Nor it is not the *ordinariness* or *extraordinariness* of the way of *making* these signs, which maketh them *currant* and *true*, or *credible*: For if God can make a *Natural false sign*, he can make a *supernatural false* one, for ought any mortal man can prove. Only all the question is, Whether it *be indeed a sign of the mind and will of God or not?* Now the *works of Nature* are Gods *Natural Signs*, and his *Natural objective Light and Law*; as the perception of them is the *Subjective*

jective or *Active Light and Law of Nature: Something* of God, these *Natural signs* do signifie or reveal *plainly*, and *some things darkly*: And so it is with *supernatural signs*; As the *written Tables*, the *voice* of an *Angel*, the *words* of an *inspired Prophet* or *Apostle*, *&c.* Now there is no other way for God to speak or reveal falsly, could he do it, but 1. Either to make a *false sign*, naturally or supernaturally, or 2. To *determine mans sense* or *mind* to a false perception. And if God can do this *naturally*, why not *supernaturally*?

Nay, *à fortiore* mark how you teach the Infidel to inferr? 1. Gods *Natural Revelations* are *Common*, and his *supernatural rare*. 2. Gods *Natural Revelations* are most *certainly* his *own Acts*: But how far a *Voice* or *Book* from a *Spirit*, may be the Act of that Spirit or Angel as a free Agent, and how far that Agent is fallible or defectible, we could not tell, if we had not farther Evidence of Gods owning it. Therefore if you make Gods own ordinary Natural Revelations or significations to be false, how will you be able to disprove the Infidel about the rest? 3. And then note, that our Case is yet lower and plainer than all this: For if the very *Being* of the Creatures, which is the *Matter* of these *Signs* be uncertain to us, and all our senses and minds deceived about it, then we have no place for enquiry, Whether this *Creature* be any sign of the mind of God. As if the *hearing* of all men was deceived, that thought they heard that voice, [*This is my Beloved Son*] or *Pauls*, that thought he heard Christ speak to him [*Saul, Saul, &c.*] or if their *Eyes* and *Intellects* were deceived, that thought they *saw Christ* and his *miracles*; or that think now that they read the Bible, and indeed there be no such thing as a Bible, no such words, *&c.* then there is no room to enquire what they

they *signifie*: For *nothing* hath *no signification*. *Truth* and *Goodness* are *affections* or modes of Being: And if we cannot by all our *sound senses* know the *Being of things*, we can much less know that they are *True or Good*. Therefore all knowledge, and all faith, and all Religion is overthrown by your denyal of the truth of our Senses and Intellects perception of things sensible.

Reason IV. And by this means you are not *capable of being disputed with*, nor any Controversie between you and any others in the world, of being decided, while you deny sense. For then you agree not with mankind in *any one common principle*. And they that agree in nothing, can dispute of nothing. For this is the first principle: *Est vel non est* is first to be agreed on, before we can dispute any farther of a *substance*. What will you do to confute an adversary, but drive him to deny a certain principle? And can you drive him to deny a *lower fundamental* Principle, than the *Being* of a *substance perceived by sense*, yea, by *all the sound senses of all men in the world*?

Reason V. Yea, it is specially to be noted, that our difference is not only about the *species* of a sensible substance, but about the very *substance it self in genere*, Whether all our senses perceive *any substance at all*, or not. Suppose the question were, Whether it be *water* or not, which all mens senses see in Rivers? If a Papist would deny it to be *water*, doubtless he denyed the agreeing judgement of all mens Intellect by sense. But if he should also say, *It is no substance*, which we call *water* or *earth*, This were to deny the *first Principle*, and most fundamental perception in nature.

Now that *this* is *your case*, is undenyable. For, 1. You profess, that *Christs Body* and *Blood* are not *sensible* there; That it is not the *quantity*, *shape*, *num-*

ber, colour, smell, weight, &c. of Christs *Body* and *Blood* which we perceive, and that these Accidents are not the Accidents of Christ. 2. And you believe that the *Bread* and *Wine* is gone, that is, changed into the body and blood of Christ; so that no part of *their* substance, matter or form is left. And you put no *third* substance under these *Accidents* in the stead. So that you maintain, that it is the *quantity of nothing*, the *figure of nothing*, the *colour*, the *weight*, the *scituation*, the *smell*, the *number, &c.* of *nothing*, which all mens Intellects by sense perceive. So that the Controversie is, *Whether it be any substance at all which by those accidents we perceive?* And when we see, handle, taste, smell it, you believe (or say you believe) that it is *none*; neither *Bread* or *Wine*, or any other: Now if by sense we cannot be sure of the *very Being of a substance*, we can be sure of nothing in the world.

Reason VI. Yea, it is to be noted, that though *Brutes* have *no Intellects*, yet their *Sense* and *Imagination* herein wholly *agreeth* with the *common perception* of *man:* A Dog or a Mouse will eat the bread as *common bread*, and a Swine will drink the Wine as *common Wine:* and therefore have the same perception of it as of common bread and wine; And so *their senses* must be all *deceived* as well as *mans*. And Brutes have as accurate perfect senses as men have, and some much more. And meer *natural operations* are more *certain* and *constant* (as we see by the worlds experience) than meer *Reason* and *Argumentation*. Birds and Beasts are constant in their perceptions and course of action, being not left to the power of *Mutable free-will*.

Reason VII. You hereby quite overthrow your own foundation, which is fetcht from *the Concord of all your party*, which you call *all the Church:* You think

profess, that *All the senses of all the sound men in the world*, and all the *simple perceptions of their Intellects by sense*, do *agree*, that there is *substance*, yea, *de specie Bread* and *Wine* after the Consecration? No *one mans* perception by sense *disagreed in this*, from the institution of the Sacrament to this day, that can be proved, or the least probability of it given. And if *this Concord* be no proof, much less is *yours*: For, 1. The Intellect in *Reasoning* is more fallible than in its *Immediate perception* of *things sensed* (or perceived by sense). 2. *Yours* is but the Consent of *some men*; but *ours* is the Consent of *all mankind*. *Yours* among your selves hath oft in Councils a *Minor part* of *dissenters*, who must be overvoted by the rest: But our Case hath *never one dissenting sense* or *perception*.

Reason VIII. By this denyal of *sense*, you overthrow the foundations of *Humane Converse*: How can men make any *sure Contracts*, or perform any *duty* on a sure ground, if the *Concordant senses* of all the world be false? Parents cannot be sure which are their own Children; nor Children which are their own Parents: Husbands cannot certainly know their own Wives from their neighbours. No Subjects can certainly know their own Prince. No man can be sure, whether he buy or sell, receive money or pay it, &c. No man can be sure that there is a Pope, or Priest, or man in the world.

Reason IX. You seem to me to *Blaspheme God*, and to make him the *greatest Deceiver of mankind*, even

which they perceive, when it is none at all.

Reason X. You thus fain God to be *Cruel to Mankind*, and that under *pretence of Grace*; Even to put such *hard Conditions of salvation* on man, which seem to us *impossible*, to any but *mad men*, or those who by faction have cast their minds into a dream. If these be *Gods Conditions*, that no man shall be *saved*, that doth not believe that all his senses, and all the senses of all the world, are deceived when they perceive *Bread and Wine*, or *substance*, many may *take on them* to believe it, but few will *believe it*, and be saved indeed.

Reason XI. Hereby you make the *Gospel* or *New Covenant* to be far *harder* and more *rigorous* than either the *Law of Moses*, or the *Law of Innocency*: For neither of these did damn men for believing the *agreeing senses of all mankind*: *Perfect Obedience*, to a perfect nature, was fit to be a delight. The burdensome Ceremonies had no such *Impossibilities* in them. None of them obliged men to renounce *all their senses*, and to come to Heaven by so hard a way.

Reason XII. You seem to me to *Contradict Gods Law and terms of life*, and to forge the *clean contrary* as his: He saith, *He that cometh to God must Believe that God is*, &c. and *He that believeth shall be saved, and he that believeth not shall be damned*: But you seem to me to say in plain effect, [*He that Believeth Gods Natural Revelations to all mens senses shall be damned*, and *that believeth that the said Revelations are false, may be saved*, cæteris paribus.]

Reason

Reaſ. XIII. And what a thing by this do you make *Gods Grace* to be? Whereas true *Grace* is the Repairer and *perfecter* of *Nature*, you make it to be the *deſtroyer* and *deceiver* of Nature. The uſe of Grace according to your faith is to cauſe men to believe that *Gods natural Revelations are falſe*, and that all the ſenſes of the world in this matter are deceived : Whereas a *mad man* can believe this *without Grace*.

Reaſ. XIV. By this doctrine you abominably corrupt the Church with *hypocriſie*, while all that will have Communion with you, muſt be forced to profeſs that all mens ſenſes are thus deceived : And can you think that *really* they *can all believe it ?* or rather your Church muſt be moſtly made up of *groſs hypocrites* who falſly take on them to believe it when they do not.

Reaſ. XV. And by this means you make the *Unity* of the Church to become a *meer Impoſſibility* : For your *condition* of *union* is, that *men all believe this among other Articles of your faith* : And that man hath loſt or vitiated his humanity who can believe and expect, that *all Chriſtians in the world ſhould ever believe that all the ſenſes of all the world are thus deceived.* You might as well ſay, The Church ſhall never have Unity till all Chriſtians do believe that *David* or *Chriſt* was a *Worm* and no *man*, a *door*, a *Vine*, a *thief*, a *Rock*, in proper ſenſe ; or we ſhall have no unity till we renounce both our *humanity* and *animality* and the *light and Law* of God in *Nature*. And after this to cry up *Unity*, and cry down *Schiſm*, what *abominable hypocriſie* is it?

Reaſ. XVI. And by this doctrine what *bloody inhumanity* is become the brand or Character of your Church? When you decree *Concil. Later. ſub. Innoc.* 3. *Can.* 3. that all that will *not thus renounce their ſenſes, and give the lie to Gods natural revelations*, ſhall be *excommunicated* and *utterly undone* in this World, even baniſhed from all that they have, and from the Land of their Nativity ; Yea your Inquiſition muſt torture and burn them, and your Writ *de hereticis comburendis* muſt be iſſued out againſt them, to fry them to death in flames, if they will not renounce the common ſenſes of mankind.

Reaſ. XVII. And it even amazeth me to think what horrid Tyrants you would thus make *all Chriſtian Princes!* When the ſaid Canon determineth that they ſhall be *firſt Excommunicate* and then caſt *out of their Dominions*, which ſhall *be given* to *others*, and their *ſubjects abſolved from their allegiance* and *fidelity*, except they will *exterminate all theſe as hereticks* from their Dominions, who will not give the lye to all mens ſenſes and to Gods natural Revelations. The plain Engliſh is, ☞ *He ſhall not be the Lord of his own Dominions who will have men to be his ſubjects*, or ſuch as will not *renounce both their humanity and animality or ſenſe*. For to *perceive ſubſtances in genere & in ſpecie* by *ſenſe*, and to *believe or truſt* the *Common ſenſes* of all *the World* about *things ſenſible*, as being the ſureſt way that we have of perception, is as *neceſſary to a Man* as *Ratiocination* is. Chooſe then O ye Princes of the Earth, whether you will be *Papiſts*, and whether you will have *no men to be your Subjects*, even *none that* believe the *ſenſes of themſelves and all the world*.

Reaſ. XVIII. Thus alſo your *Idolatry* exceedeth in abſurdity the *Idolatry* of all the Heathens elſe in the World : Even Canibals and the moſt barbarous Nations upon Earth. For if they call men to Worſhip an Image, the Sun, the Moon, an Ox or an Onion (of which the Egyptians are accuſed) they do but ſay that ſome *ſpiritual* or *celeſtial numen* affixeth his *operative preſence* to this Creature : But they never make men *ſwear* that *there is no Image*, or *Sun* or *Moon* or *Ox* or *Onion* left, but that the *whole substance* of it is turned into God, or somewhat else. Your Absurdities tend to make the grossest Idolatry seem comparatively to yours, a very fair and tolerable errour.

Reas. XIX. By these means you expose *Christianity* to the *scorn* of *humane nature*, and all the world. You teach Heathens, Mahometans and other Infidels to deride Christ as we do *Mahomet*; and to say that a Christian *Maketh* and *Eateth his God*, and his faith is a *Believing that Gods supernatural Revelations are a lie*, and that God *is like the Devil the great Deceiver of the world*. Wo be to the world because of offences, and wo be to him by whom offence cometh.

Reas. XX. Lastly by this means you are the grand pernicious hinderers of the Conversion of the Heathen and Infidel world: For you do as it were proclaim to them; [*Never turn Christians till you will believe that Gods Natural Revelations are false, and that all mens senses in the world are deceived, in judging that there is Bread, Wine, or sensible substance after the words of Consecration.*]

These are the mischievous Consequents of your doctrine. But one benefit I confess doth come by occasion of it; that it is easier hereby to *believe* that there *are Devils*, when we see how they can deceive men: and to *believe* the *evil of sin*, when we see how it maketh men mad; and to *believe* that there is a *Hell*, when we see such a Hell already on Earth, as Learned Pompous Clergie men, that have studied to attain this malignant madness to decree to fry men in the flames and damn them to Hell, and give them no peace or quietness in the World, unless they will say, that Gods Natural Revelations are false, and that all mens senses are herein deceived, by God as the great deceiver of the World.

P. IT is easie to make any cause seem odious, till the accusations are answered, which I shall confidently do in the present case.

I. All this is but argument from sense: And sense must vail to *faith:* Gods word must be believed before our senses.

R. It is easie to cheat fools and children into a dream, with a sound of empty words: To talk of *senses vailing to faith* and such like Canting, and insignificant words, may serve turn with that sort of men. But sober men will tell you that *sense* is in *exercise* in order of *Nature* at least before *Reason* or *faith*, and that we are *Men* and *Animals before* we are *Christians:* And that the *truth* and *certainty of faith*, presupposeth the *Truth* and *Certainty* of *sense.* Tell me else, if sense be false, how you know that there is a *Man*, or *Pope*, or *Priest* in the World? that there is a *Book* or *Voice*, or any being? And what *possibility* then have you of *Believing?*

P. Gods Revelation is surer than our senses?

R. This is the old song over and over. Revelation without sense (to you and ordinary Christians at least) is a contradiction. How know you that God hath any revelations? If by *preachers words*, How know you that there is a *preacher*, or a *word* but by sense? If by *books*, How know you that there *is a book*, but by sense?

P. II. We may trust sense in all other things, where

God

because God forbiddeth us.

R. Say so of your Church too, your Pope, Council or Traditions; that we may trust them in all cases save one or two, in which it is certain that they do lye! And will not any man conclude, that he that can lye in one case, can lye in more? If one Text of Gods word were false, and you would say, You may believe all the rest save that, how will you ever prove it? For the formal object of faith is gone, which is the *Divine Veracity*; He that can lye once, can lye twice. So if all our senses be false in this instance, how shall we know that hey are ever true?

P. You may know it because God saith it.

R. 1. Where doth God say it? 2. How shall I be ure that he saith it? If you say, that it is written in Scripture; besides that there is no such word; How hall I know that all mens senses are not deceived in hinking that there is a *Scripture*, or such a word in t? If you say that the *Council* saith it, How shall I now that there is a *man* or ever was a *Council*, or a Book in the world? The certainty of *Conclusions* preupposeth the certainty of *premises* and *principles:* And he certainty of *faith* and *Reasoning*, presupposeth the ertainty of sense: And if you deny this, you deny all, nd in vain plead for the rest.

P. I must believe my senses, where I have no reason o disbelieve them. But when God contradicteth them, have reason to disbelieve them.

R. 1. You vainly suppose without proof that God ontradicteth them. So you may say, I may or must elieve the Scripture or an Apostle, Prophet or Miracle, xcept God contradict them. But if God contradict hem, he contradicteth his own word or revelation: or we have no other from him, but by man: And if he contradict

contradict himself, or his own word, how can I believe him, or know which of his words it is thats true, when one is false ? so here : His *Natural Revelation* is his *first*, *nearest*; and most *satisfactory revelation* : And if that be said to be false by his *supernatural revelation*, which shall I believe, and why ?

P. III. You cannot deny but God *can* deceive our senses. And therefore if he *can*, will you conclude against all faith if once he do it ?

R. 1. This is not *once*; but as oft as God is worshiped in your Mass and our Sacrament.

2. God can *deceive* us without a *Lie*, but not *by a Lie*. *Christ deceived* the two Disciples, *Luke* 24. by carrying it *as if he would* have gone further; but not by *saying* that he *would go further*. God can do that from which he knoweth that man will take *occasion* of deceit. God can blind a mans eyes, or destroy or corrupt his other senses; he can present an object defectively, with unmeet mediums, distance, site, *&c*. In this case he doth not give us a FALSE SIGN; nor doth he by the Nature of the Revelation oblige any man to believe it : Yea *Nature* saith, that a man is not to Judge by a *vitiated sense*, or an *unmeet medium*, or a *too distant object*, or where the due qualification of the sense or object are wanting : *Nature* there tells us that we are there to suppose or suspect that we are uncapable of certainty : But *Nature obligeth* us to believe *sound senses* about *duly qualified objects*; and to take *sense* for *sound* when all the *senses* of all the *men in the world agree*; and the object to be a duly qualified object of sense, when all mens senses in the world so perceive it. For we have no way but by sense to know what is an object of sense.

3. The question is not what God *can* do by his *power*, if he will; but what God *will do*, and *can will* to

istency with his *perfection*, and just and
rnment of the World. And God in ma-
hose Intellects are naturally to perceive
by the means of the perception of sense,
oblige man and *necessitate* him also, to
in such perception. And in *Nature* man
way of apprehension: Therefore if you
at sense is *ordinarily fallible*, and Gods
it *false*, yet man were not only *allowed*
to *use* and *trust it*, as having *no better*
pprehension: As among *many knaves* or
most trust the *honestest* and *most trusty*,
s better to trust. If I am not sure that it
ht that I see, yet I am sure that I must
ption of it as a *Sun* or *Light* as it is;
given me no better. If I am not sure
feeling, taste, *&c.* are infallible; yet I
am made of God to *use them*; and that
senses, nor a better way to be certain
objects: so that I must take and trust
e, or cease to be a man.
ists Body and Blood are not sensible ob-
refore sense is no proper judge whether

ne of your gross kind of cheats, to change
We are not yet come to the question,
s Body and blood be here? And I grant you
o judge of that, any more than whether
re. But the question is now only, Whe-
Vine or *sensible substance* be here? And
no natural way but by sense to judge.
od should say to you [*Your senses are in
Here is no bread or wine or sensible sub-*
d you not believe him?

R. 1. Again

R. 1. Again I tell you, it is a ſuppoſition not to be put: As if you ſhould ſay, [*If God ſhould ſay,* that *part of the Goſpel* or *word of God is falſe, would you not believe him?*] 2. If I know that God telleth me that ſome diſeaſe or falſe medium, *&c.* deceive *me* or *another* in *particular*, I will believe him: But here it is ſuppoſed, 1. That I have aſſurance that it is God that tells me ſo; 2. And that I have no aſſurance that *common ſenſe* ſaith the contrary. *But* if the *ſenſe of all the world* about a well ſcituate object of ſenſe agree, I will not take that to be *Gods word* which contradicteth it, till I have *ſome evidence* which is *better* and *ſtronger* than the *agreeing ſenſes of all the world* to prove it to be ſo. And what evidence muſt that be? I aſſure you ſomewhat greater than the authority of a beaſtly ignorant murdering Pope, and his factious Council.

P. VI. *Carteſius* giveth you an inſtance of deception of ſight: We think a ſquare Tower of a Steeple to be round till we come neer it: And the water ſeemeth to us to move when it is the boat.

R. Carteſius and you do ſeem to be Confederate, to put out the eye of nature, and tempt the world to Infidelity, if not to Atheiſm. 1. *Nature* tells us that a *diſtant Steeple* or other object, is not perfectly *diſcernible:* and therefore *Nature* forbiddeth us to judge till we come neerer. We ſpeak only of *objects duly ſcituate* and *qualified.* 2. The failing of the ſight there is but *Negative:* It *diſcerneth not the corners:* but here you feign it to be *poſitive.* 3. As the errour is corrigible by *nearer approach,* ſo alſo by the uſe of *other ſenſes.* If a man *feel* the Tower that is *ſquare,* he will infallibly perceive it. But if you could prove that this ſquare Tower is no *Tower,* no *Stone,* no *Subſtance at all,* though all *the world* ſhould judge otherwiſe that ſee it at the

meeteſt

meeteſt diſtance, and *feel* it with their hands, then you did ſomething to the purpoſe.

So as to the moving water or banks, 1. Motion is not ſo evident as *ſubſtance*. 2. Though *one ſenſe*, through the weakneſs of the brain be inſufficient, the *Intellect* by the *ſame ſenſe* about other objects, and by *other ſenſes* can *infallibly diſcern* what that one perceiveth not. 3. And if one mans eyes deceive him who is in the *boat*, *ten thouſand mens* eyes that ſtand on the *firm land*, perceive the truth: But in our caſe it is all the ſenſes of all the world, in all ages, about the *neereſt object*, that agree.

P. VII. *Subſtance* is not the proper object of *ſenſe*, but only *Accidents*: We ſee, feel, taſte, ſmell the accidents, but not the ſubſtances.

R. 1. If you can name ſome notional ſpeculator or *Word-maker* that hath ſaid ſo, you think you have *authority* to renounce *humanity* by it. Call it *proper* or *not-proper*, *ſubſtance* is the certain *object of ſenſe* as cloathed with its accidents. *Quantity* and the *res quanta* are not two *things*, but one: And he that feeleth or ſeeth *quantity*, feeleth or ſeeth the *rem quantam*. He that ſeeth or feeleth ſhape or figure, ſeeth or feeleth the thing figured. He that ſmelleth odor, ſmelleth *rem odoratam*; He that ſeeth Colour, ſeeth the *rem coloratam*. When to feel the ſuperficies, you feel the ſubſtance.

2. By this we ſee how by *words* you will unman mankind. Have you *any way of perception* of *corporal ſubſtances* but *by ſenſe*? Do you *know* that there is *any Earth or Water*, or any *corporal ſubſtance* in the world, or not? If you do, tell us *how* you know it but by the perception of ſenſe preſenting it to the Intellect? You *know* that you muſt *thus know it*, or not at all.

3. And thus ſtill you would bring men with Scepti-

cifm to Infidelity. You would teach men, that the that faw Chrift were not fure that they faw him or an fubftance at all, but only the accidents, called Quantity Shape, Colour, &c. They that faw Apoftles, Miracles Bibles, Councils, were not fure that they faw any mor than accidents, &c.

P. VIII. They that faw Angels appearing to ther like men, or the Holy Ghoft defcending on Chrift i the fhape of a Dove, thought they faw *Men* and Dove: So *Mofes* Rod did feem a Serpent. But thei fenfes did deceive them.

R. Their fenfes were not at all deceived: And if by rafh judging they would go *beyond fenfe*, and wilfully deceive themfelves, it was their fault. Their fenfe faw the *fhape* or *likenefs* of a *man* and *dove*. The text faith not that the Holy Ghoft was a *dove*, but that it *defcended in the likenefs of a Dove*: and their fenfes perceived no more. And this was true. A man confifteth of a foul and a body of flefh and blood: Did fenfe perceive any of this in the Angels? either, foul, flefh or blood; or any fuch thing in the appearance of a *dove*? If I fee your picture or ftatue, is my fenfe deceived if I take it not for *a living man*? If I fee it *moved*, is my fenfe deceived if I take it not for any other than a *moving Image*? Nature doth not bind me to take every *fimile* to be *idem*; a *corps* for a *man*; an *Image* for the *perfon*. It will be foolifhnefs fo to take it. But if this *Angel*, or *Dove*, had come near to the *fenfes*, all *the fenfes*, of all forts of men, and they had *feen*, and *felt*, and *tafted*, and *fmelt*, all that are the objects of thefe fenfes, and yet there had been indeed no vifible, tactible, fenfible *fubftance at all*, this had been a deception of the fenfes remedilefs. Chrift I am fure appealed to fenfe, to prove that he had flefh and blood and was not a meer fpirit. The fame I fay of *Mofes* Rod: either it was really a Serpent or not; If it was, then it was no deception to judge it such: If not, sense was not at all deceived: For it perceived nothing but the similitude and motion, and those (with the substance) were certainly there. But if all mens senses, seeing, feeling, tasting, *&c.* had been deceived, and there had been indeed no *shape* of a Serpent, nor any *sensible substance* at all but Accidents real without any substance, this had been indeed a deception of the senses. And if God so subvert mans nature, he will not bind him to do the things which belong to the nature of man to do.

But by all this we may perceive, that there is no end of Controversies with you to be hoped for: For how is it possible to bring any thing to a more satisfying issue, than when the senses of all the world do as clearly perceive it, as any sensible thing can be perceived? If our difference were whether this be Paper, and these be Letters; or whether this be a Pen, a Table, yea or a substance, and I should appeal to the sense of all the World, and yet this will not serve to decide the Controversie; what end, or hope of ending can there be: I will sooner look for concord with a mad man, than with men that deny the senses of all the World.

CHAP.

CHAP. III.

The second Argument against Transubstantiation: The Contradictions of it.

R. *Arg.* 2. GOd owneth not Contradictions (nor can do). The Papists doctrine of Transubstantiation, or nullification of the whole substance of Bread and Wine, is contradictious: Therefore it is not owned by God.

The Major I know no man that denyeth.

The Contradictions are these.

I. You feign many *Accidents* of *no substance*; which is a gross contradiction. For to be an *Accident* is essentially *Relative* to a subject or substance: And *ejus esse est inesse*. To be a *Father* without a Son, or a Son without a Father, a Husband without a Wife, or a Wife without a Husband, *&c.* are contradictions: And so it is to be an *Accident of nothing*, or without a *subject*.

Particularly, 1. The *quantity of nothing* is a contradiction: We can *measure* the Bread, and Wine: To be an *inch* in longitude, latitude or profundity, and yet to be *no substance* is a contradiction. To be (as the Wine is) a *quart*, a *gallon* of *Nothing* is a contradiction.

2. So for *number*; we can number the *wafers* or *pieces* of Bread, and the *Cups* of Wine: And to be *twenty*, *forty*, an *hundred nothings*, is a contradiction.

3. So for the *Weight*, To be an *ounce*, a *pound*, or *ten pound*, of *nothing*, is a contradiction.

4. So for the *figure* or *shape*: It is a contradiction to be a *round nothing*, a *square nothing*, &c.

5. So is it to be a *sweet nothing*, a *sharp nothing*, an *austere nothing*, *&c.* as the *Wine* is fancied by you.

6. Or to be an *odoriferous nothing*: A *rough* or a *smooth nothing*, &c.

7. Or to be a *white nothing*, or a *red nothing*, or any coloured *nothing*. The same I may say of *site*, and of a multitude of Relations, *&c.*

II. It is a contradiction, for *Nothing* to have all those *Real notable effects*, which it is certain that the consecrated *Bread* and *Wine* have.

As, 1. That when a man or a beast, is *really nourished* by the *Bread* and *Wine*, and *flesh* and *blood*, and *spirits* are made of it, (as they may live by it many months,) that these should be the *effects* of *nothing*, or made out of *no substance* by way of *Nutrition*, without a proper Creation.

2. When the Consecrated *Bread* and *Wine* do partly turn to *Excrements*, *Urine*, *Dung* and *Spittle*, that all the Excrements are *nothings* or *made of nothing* without a *new Creation*, is a contradiction.

3. When the *Wine* shall (as it may do) make a *man* or a *swine drunk*, that he is made *drunk* by *nothing* or no *substance*, when as that *drunkenness* is essentially the operation of the spirits of the *Wine* upon the spirits of him that drinks it, this also is a contradiction. And God maketh not contradictions true.

P. It is the plea of an Infidel to say that *God* cannot do this or that. Will you limit the power of the Almighty? Will you say that God *cannot* make Quantity, quality, site, *&c.* without substance, because we cannot? It is blasphemy to say God cannot.

R. God *can* do All things that are *works of Power*: God *can do nothing* which is a work of *Impotency*, *defectiveness*, *naughtiness*, or *folly*, or which are contradictions in themselves. And when we say *God cannot*, we do but say either that God is *Perfect* and *Almighty*, or that the thing is *Nothing*, but a false name, and not capable of being any ones work. God *cannot lye*, because he is perfect and Almighty, and not because he wanteth power. God cannot make you to be a *man* and *no man*, a *substance* and *no substance*, in the same sence, at the same time: because it is a contradiction.

But if this Argument did not hold, and it were no contradiction, for God to overturn his setled course of Nature, I shall shew you next that we have other reasons enough to judge that he doth it not. If he *Can* make darkness to give Light, and a clod to be to the World instead of the Sun, without changing it, or a stone to understand and speak without changing it, yet that God *doth* none of this, both reason and experience prove.

CHAP.

The Third Argument against Transubstantiation: from the certain falshood of their assertion of multitudes of Miracles in it.

R. THat doctrine which asserteth a multitude of false or feigned Miracles is false and not of God: But such is the doctrine of Transubstantiation—*Ergo*——

I will 1. Shew you what Miracles it asserteth; and 2. Prove that they are feigned or false.

I. It is a Miracle for *Bread* and *Wine* to be turned into no *Bread* and *Wine*, yea, into *nothing*; and this by the *speaking* of *four words*.

II. It is a Miracle (or Contradiction) for the Bread and Wine to be turned into *Christs Body* and *Blood*, and yet neither the *matter* nor *form* of it to become any of the matter of Christs body and blood.

III. It is a Miracle, (or a contradiction rather as aforesaid) for the Accidents to be the Accidents of *Nothing*, or no *substance*; to be the *quantity* of *Nothing*, the *shape*, the *number* of *nothing*, the *colour*, *savour*, *smell* of nothing, and so of all the rest.

IV. It is a Miracle to have all the sound senses of all sorts of men in the world so deceived herein, as to perceive *bread*, *wine* and *substance*, if there be none.

V. It is a Miracle to have the senses of Mice and Rats, and Dogs and other Brutes also deceived when they eat and drink it.

VI. It is a Miracle (or contradiction) to have *nothing* without a Creation, to become *excrements*: or else those *excrements* to be *nothing* also: And the

Accidents of all those *excrements* to be the *Accidents of Nothing*.

VII. It is a Miracle to be *nourished* by *Nothing*: (For you say, that it is not *Christs body* and *blood* that nourisheth the flesh.) To have flesh and blood made of *nothing*, is a creation.

VIII. It is a Miracle to be *drunk* with *nothing*, when the *Wine* is annihilated or gone, and *seemeth* to be it that causeth the effect: Yea, for Beast or man to be so drunk.

IX. It is a Miracle (or contradiction) for Christ to eat his own body (as the Papists hold he did); and yet it was his *Whole Body* which did eat his *body*, and yet he had but one body.

X. It was a Miracle (or contradiction) for *Christs* entire body to be nourished by that eaten body, and that the eaten body turned into the substance of his eating body: And yet all was but one.

XI. It was a Miracle that Christs *Eaten body* being not dead but living with a humane soul, should be broken and eaten by him and his disciples, and yet feel no pain by it.

XII. It was a Miracle that his whole body was on the Cross; and yet part of it in the disciples bellies at that time; or at least before that eaten by them.

XIII. It was a Miracle (or contradiction) that Christs eaten body now nourisheth not the flesh of any man; and yet did nourish the flesh of the disciples before his death. Or if it did not nourish them, it was a Miracle that what they eat and drank then did not nourish them, (or Christ what he eat and drank).

XIV. It was a Miracle that the whole body of Christ should arise and live, and ascend to Heaven, when the disciples had eaten it.

XV. It is a Miracle that every Receiver eateth the whole body of Chriſt, and not a part, and yet that he hath but one body; or that they eat each a part without dividing him.

XVI. It is a Miracle that as ſoon as the ſpecies of *Bread* and *Wine* periſh or ceaſe in the Eater, Chriſts body and blood ceaſeth to be in him, and this without his detriment.

XVII. It is a Miracle that there is ſuch a local diſtance between the conſecrated bread and wine all over the world; and yet no ſuch diſtance between the parts of Chriſts body, and yet that bread to be his body.

XVIII. It is a Miracle that bread and wine is Annihilated or ceaſe every Maſs, and yet that the quantity of corporeal matter in the whole world is no whit diminiſhed: or elſe that thoſe four words can ſo annihilate and diminiſh the matter of the world.

XIX. It is a Miracle that Chriſts body and blood increaſe not, when ſo many millions of parcells of bread and wine are turned into it.

XX. It is a Miracle that Chriſts body and blood is not diminiſhed, when by the Corruption of the ſpecies of bread and wine, it vaniſheth away.

XXI. It is a Miracle that Chriſts body and blood ſhould be ſo received into the bowels of a wicked man, and yet not be any way defiled by his ſin, nor by his bodily uncleanneſs.

XXII. It is a Miracle that a Baker diſpoſitively, and a Prieſt effectually can make his own God, and eat him when they have done.

XXIII. It is a Miracle that when Worms are bred of that which was bread and wine, theſe worms are really generated of *nothing*, or created; (or if as ſome ſay, the bread and wine do ſubſtantially return again, and breed them, that is another, a double miracle.)

XXIV. And it is a Miracle that the Corporeal matter of the world should by these Worms be daily increased, out of nothing, or out of meer accidents that have no substance.

XXV. It is a Miracle that men may be poysoned by the Sacramental Elements as ingredients in the mixture, and yet that they are no substance.

XXVI. It is a Miracle or Contradiction, that when *flesh* and *blood* (formally such) enter not into the Kingdom of God, but Glorified bodies are all *spiritual bodies* (though not Spirits), and therefore not *flesh* and *blood*: Yet Christs *body* in the Sacrament should be truly and properly *flesh* and *blood*, and yet the same with his glorified body (which is not flesh and blood:) which is the Papists doctrine; and the bread turned into such flesh.

XXVII. It is a Miracle that the same *Body* which in Heaven is brighter in Glory than the Sun, and exalted above Angels, should yet shew no signs of Glory on the Altar, in the Cup, in the hand, mouth or belly of him that taketh it; but all its Glory be so hid.

XXVIII. It is a Miracle (or Contradiction) that Christs Humiliation should be past, and his whole Body Glorified, and yet that to be torn with the teeth of a wicked man, to be eaten by Mice, Rats or Dogs, to go into the filthy guts, to be trodden in the dirt, should be neither painful, nor any diminution of the Glory of that same body. Indeed his body on the Cross might be broken, and his blood spilt and trodden on, because he was a sacrifice for sin; and it was the time of his Voluntary Humiliation: But now for the suffering of death he is crowned with Glory and Honour, *Heb.* 2. 9, 7.

XXIX. It is a Miracle that the *Living Body* of our Glorified Redeemer should give no evidence or sign of

life:

life; neither ſtir, nor ſpeak, nor have breath, pulſe, warmth, or other property of life appearing.

XXX. It is a Miracle, at leaſt, that *fleſh* ſhould have none of the common notes or properties of fleſh, not to be made of food, of blood and chyme, not to conſiſt of the *fibræ* which fleſh conſiſteth of; not to have the colour, taſte, odour or other ſuch accidents of fleſh: And that Blood ſhould have none of theſe notifying accidents of *blood*.

XXXI. It is a Miracle or Contradiction, that *Chriſts Fleſh* was *Broken* before it was broken, ſacrificed before it was ſacrificed, I mean really broken and ſacrificed at his Supper, when yet he was whole and not really ſacrificed till he was nailed to the Croſs. And ſo that his blood was really and properly ſhed in his Supper, and yet no skin broken, nor his blood really ſhed till his ſide was pierced on the Croſs. And that he that was but *once offered* and *ſacrificed*, ſhould yet be offered and ſacrificed once on one day, and another time on another day.

Here are one and thirty Miracles or Contradictions: Let us hear ſome of the Aggravations of them, as worthy to be conſidered.

I. It is a Miracle of theſe Miracles, that there ſhould be as many Miracle workers as Prieſts in the world: How many thouſand are they in *France* alone? And ſo in many other Countreys. Whereas in Chriſts own time, they were comparatively but few.

II. That the Pope or any Prelate can make a Miracle worker when he pleaſe, yea, a thouſand; as if the Holy Ghoſt were at his will.

III. It is a Miracle of theſe Miracles that a Simoniſt who buyeth the Prieſthood with money, doth buy the Holy Ghoſt to work Miracles for that money, which *Simon Magus* was condemned for thinking poſſible.

For the Papists hold, that the Consecration of a Simoniacal Priest transubstantiateth.

IV. It is a Miracle that all this power of Miracles should be given to flagitious wicked men; Adulterers, Murderers, Drunkards, *&c.*

V. It is a Miracle that all these men can work Miracles at their *own will and pleasure*, at any hour: whereas the Apostles had not the Spirit at command, and could not do it when they would.

VI. It is a Miracle that Miracles should be as common as Masses, or the Eucharistical worshipping of God; 'not only on every Lords Day in all Church-assemblies, but any day or hour else in the Week. And so Miracles be as ordinary almost as to eat and drink.'

VII. It is a Miracle that every wicked Priest should do so *many Miracles in one*, and so many more in number than *Christ himself* did, in the same proportion of time, as far as the History of the Gospel telleth us: Christ is quite exceeded by them all.

VIII. It is a Miracle that every wicked Priest can work all these Miracles *so easily*, as with the careless saying over *four words*: When the *Apostles* could not cast out some Devils, or work some Miracles, and some could not be done but by *fasting and prayer.*

IX. It is a Miracle that *every Priest* can work all these Miracles upon an *unbeliever* or a *wicked* man: For to such they say, it is the *real flesh and blood of Christ*, and *no bread or wine*; And the *senses* of all these *wicked men* are deceived. Whereas Christ himself *could not do any great miraculous work* among some where he came, *because of their unbelief.*

X. It is a Miracle that *God and the Priest* should do these foresaid Miracles on *Mice and Rats* and other *Beasts*, by deceiving their senses, which we find not that

that Christ ever did: or that God should feed them with the miraculous accidents aforesaid.

XI. It is a Miracle of these Miracles that the Priest can thus easily work Miracles not only on *other creatures*, but on the *glorified body of Christ himself*, (by the foresaid changes, *&c.*)

XII. It is a Miracle, that when Christ wrought his Miracles usually before a far smaller number, these Priests work Miracles thus before or on the *senses of all the men in the world* that will be present at the Mass; for all their senses are deceived.

XIII. It is a Miracle that the Abassines, Armenians, Greeks, Protestants, yea, any that they call Schismaticks, and Hereticks, who do not intend to work any Miracle, nor believe Transubstantiation, do yet work Miracles in each Sacramental administration of the Eucharist, not only *without* their *knowledge*, but *contrary* to *their belief*, and *against their wills:* For they say, that even such mens consecration is effectual.

Vid. Aquin. 3. q. 82. a. 7. c.

XIV. Either their Priests consecration worketh all these Miracles, when they *intend it not*, (as if they speak the words in jeast or scorn, or in Infidelity,) or only when they *intend it*. If the first be said, it is a Miracle of Miracles, that any Priest can work so many and great Miracles by a jeast or scorn——If not, then all the business is come to nothing, and no one but the Priest knoweth whether there be any such Miracle at all, and whether ever he eat the flesh of Christ: And so it will be in the power of the Priest to deceive and damn all the people, according to the Papists exposition of Christs words, Joh. 6. *Except ye eat the flesh of the Son of man and drink his blood, you have no life in you.*

Vid. Aquin. 3. q. 69. a. 9.

XV.

XV. Either a malicious intention to a wrong end will be effectual in Consecration, or not. If not, none but the Priest knoweth that there is any body and blood of Christ, or that ever he received any: Because none knoweth though the Priest intend Consecration, whether he intend it to a right end. But if a wicked end will serve (as I think most of them hold) the Miracle may be great and sad. For any Roguish drunken malicious Priest may undo a Baker or Vintner at his pleasure, and by four words deprive him of all his Bread and Wine : Yea, he might nullifie all the *Bread and Wine* in the *City*, and so either make a famine at his pleasure, or else make *whole Families* and *Cities* live still and be nourished without *any substance* by bare *Accidents*, which would be a *Miracle* indeed.

If the Priest can by consecration change *only a convenient quantity of bread and wine* , then all that is *overmuch* is *bread and wine* after consecration. If otherwise, why may he not change all the bread and wine in the Shop or Cellar where he cometh, intending consecration to an ill end?

If he can do it only on the *Altar* , then want of *an Altar* would frustrate the effect (which they hold not). But if he can do it *without an Altar* he may do it in the *Shop and Cellar*.

If he can do it only on the *bread and wine present*, how *near* must it be? Then the words will work *at so many* yards distance, and not at *so many*. Or if he cannot do it *out of sight*, a *blind Priest* cannot do it. But if he can do it on that which is *absent* , we may fear lest in an anger he may take away all the bread and wine in the Land ; at least in a frolick to try his power.

XVI. And it is some aggravaion of these manifold Miracles that a *Degraded Priest* can do them: Because they follow the indelible Character: And so he that hath once made a Miracle-worker, cannot take away his power again, nor his *sin* lose his *power*. Is not this a marvellous power of Miracles, which becometh like a *nature* to them, as the power of speaking is?

Vid. Aquin. 3. q. 82. a. 8.

XVII. Yet is this Miracle-working-power more miraculous, in that a mans own *unwillingness*, or *Repentance* of his Calling cannot hinder the Miracle if he do but speak four words. *Consent* it *self* is not necessary to it: Let a man *Repent* that ever he was *a Priest*, and profess that he continueth in that Calling against his will, yea, let him write as I now do *against Transubstantiation*, yet all this will not hinder his next Consecration from working all the foresaid Miracles.

XVIII. It is miraculous that if you keep a consecrated Wafer never so long, if you use it never so coursly, if you (as he did who occasioned the conversion of Mr. *Anthony Egan* a late *Irish* Priest) pawn it at an Ale-house for thirty shillings; if you lay it down for a stake at Cards or Dice, *&c.* it will not *cease* to be *Christs flesh* (and so by his blood,) nor ever becomes bread, or any other substance till it *corrupt*: And yet in a mans stomach it ceaseth to be Christs body, as natural heat corrupteth it by concoction: And yet it is not *Christs flesh* that is concocted.

XIX. It is a Miracle of this Miracle which *Aquinas* and others assert, that the Bread and Wine are not *Annihilated*, but wholly turned into Christs body and blood; and yet, as *Vasquez* saith, *It is not that the matter of bread begins to be under the form of Christs body* (as *Durandus* held.) Saith *Veron Reg. fid. cap.* 5.

[This

This *Transubstantiation is neither a change nor a production of any thing; but it is a Relation of order between the substance that doth desist to be, and that into which it doth desist.* And yet saith the *Concil. Trident. There is a change made of the whole substance into,* &c.

XX. Lastly, It is a Miracle that all these Miracles should be done so as not to *appear* to the senses of any man living, either to Convert Unbelievers or Confirm the faithful: So that millions of these Miracles are *seen* and *not seen*; the Priest, and Action, and Accidents are *seen*, but no Miracle seen by any. So that *Aquinas* concludeth 3. *q.* 76. *a*, 7, [Though Christ be existent in this Sacrament *per modum substantiæ*, yet neither *bodily eyes*, nor *our Intellects* can see him, but by *faith*: no nor the *Intellect of an Angel* can see him *secundum sua naturalia*; nor do Devils see him but by faith; nor the blessed, but in the Divine Essence.]

All these make these Miracles far more miraculous than the raising of *Lazarus* from the dead.

WHether all these are Miracles, or most or many of them Contradictions, and therefore Impossibilities, I make no great matter of at this time. I think it utterly needless to add any more to what is said in answer to such sayings as *Aquinas*'s (3. q. 75. & 76.) and other Schoolmen, that [*The senses are not deceived, because there are the Accidents, and the Intellect is by faith preserved from deception: that the remaining accidents are* in quantitate dimensiva quasi in subjecto: *that these Accidents can change an extrinsick body, can be corrupted, can generate Worms, can nourish, can be broken,* &c.] For all this at least confesseth, that its all done by Miracle; (Though I will

will say, 1. That they could scarce have chosen a more unhappy pro-subject of Accidents than Quantity, nor have given more unhappy reasons for it than *Aquinas* doth q. 77. a. 2. c. 1. *Because the sense perceiveth that it is* Aliquid quantum, *that is coloured.* 2. *Because Quantity is the first disposition of matter*, &c. For this includeth *matter*: and *Aliquid quantum* is a word that giveth away his Cause: And no Accident is more the same with its subject than *Quantity*, or *moles extensiva.* 2. And he will be long before he will make or prove mans nature to be such, as that his Intellect can judge of substances by Believing, as incomplex objects, before it have *perceived them* by sense and imagination. When we see, taste, smell, feel, hear them, the Intellect will suddenly and necessarily have some *species* or *perception* of the *Thing*, before it come *Logically* to dispute from *extrinsick media* of Testimony, What this thing is in a second notion. And our question is, Whether the Intellect in *this first Perception* be deceived, or not? If you discharge the Intellect from *perceiving* substances presently, before it know them by second notions or Argument, you will make man quite another thing, than every hour and action tells us he is: But what will not a man say, when he sets himself only to study what to say for the making good of his undertaken Cause?

But my next work is to prove the Falshood of these pretended Miracles.

CHAP.

CHAP. V.

The Minor proved, viz. *That these Miracles are false.*

THat these are all but feigned Miracles, I thus prove. I. Because the holy Scriptures do plainly deny such an ordinariness or commonness of the gift of Miracles. 1 Cor. 12. 8, 9, 10, 11. [*To one is given by the spirit the word of Wisdom, to another the word of Knowledge by the same spirit, to another faith by the same spirit, to another the gifts of healing by the same spirit, to another the working of miracles,* &c. *But all these worketh that one and the self same spirit; dividing to every man severally as he will.* 28, 29. *And God hath set some in the Church, first Apostles, secondarily Prophets, thirdly Teachers, after that miracles, then gifts of healing, helps, Governments, diversities of tongues: Are all Apostles? are all Prophets? are all Teachers? are all workers of Miracles.*]

Here it is most expresly told us, that working Miracles is a peculiar gift of some, and even in those times not common to all that were Priests. But the Papists make it common to every Priest, though a common Adulterer, Drunkard, Murderer or Heretick; no one Priest in the world is without it.

II. Though some few that were workers of iniquity might have some such gifts, *Matth.* 7. Yet that was so rare, that Nature it self taught men to judge Miracles to be signs of divine approbation: so that *Nicodemus* thence argueth, Joh. 3. 2. *No man could do these Miracles that thou dost except God be with him.* And the he man *Joh.* 9. 31. *God heareth not ſinners, but if any man be a Worſhipper of God and doth his will, him he heareth.* And the people, verſ. 16. *How can a man that is a ſinner do ſuch Miracles?* And it was Chriſts own proof that he was of *God*, and his *Goſpel true*; and therefore to *Blaſpheam his Miracles*, by aſcribing them to the *Devil*, was the *unpardonable Blaſphemy* of the *Holy Ghoſt*: And to deny *Miracles* to be a ſign of *Gods atteſtation* is to ſubvert all Chriſtianity. Act. 2. 22. *Jeſus of* Nazareth *a man approved of God among you by miracles, wonders and ſigns which God did by him in the midſt of you* — Joh. 5. 36. *The ſame works that I do bear witneſs of me that the Father hath ſent me.* Joh. 10. 25, 37, 38. *The works that I do in my Fathers name, they bear witneſs of me* —— *If I do not the works of my Father, believe me not: But if I do, though ye believe not me, believe the works, that ye may know and believe that the Father is in me, and I in him.*

Joh. 14. 11. *Believe me for the very works ſake.*

Joh. 15. 24. *If I had not done among them the works that no other man did, they had not had ſin.*

This alſo was *Pauls* proof of his Apoſtleſhip, yea and of the truth of all the Apoſtles doctrine: Heb. 2. 3, 4. *God alſo bearing them witneſs both with ſigns and wonders, and divers Miracles, and gifts of the Holy Ghoſt, according to his own Will.*

2 Cor. 12. 12. Rom. 15. 19. Act. 14. 3. & 15. 12.

Therefore that Doctrine is unlike to be true, which tells us that *every wicked Prieſt in the world*, though a *Simoniſt*, or an *enemy of Chriſt* and *Godlineſs*, and *drown'd in all Vice*, is ſuch a *conſtant miracle-worker*: When *God hateth all the workers of iniquity*, Pſal. 5. 5.

Matth. 21. 15.

III. But though this Reason be but *probable*, this following is *demonstrative* to a *believer*.

That doctrine which maketh every Ignorant wicked or Heretical Priest in the world, far to excell the Prophets, Apostles, and Christ himself, in the Greatness, Number and facility of Miracles, is false : But such is this doctrine of Transubstantiation ——

I know that Christ telleth his Apostles [*Greater works than these shall ye do.*] But. 1. There are *Greater works* (such as the converting of greater numbers in the world) which are not *Greater Miracles* : 2. And what was promised to the *Apostles*, as to *Miracles*, was not promised to *every Priest* in the world.

I appeal to the Consciences of sober Christians, whether it sound not as an arrogant if not blaspheamous speech, to say that *Christ and his Apostles did fewer and smaller miracles* (proportionable to their time) *than every Priest*.

And as to the Minor, it is soon proved in its parts.

1. As to the *Greatness* of the *Miracles* ; those of Christ were *exceeding Great* : especially his *Raising Lazarus*, and his *own Resurrection*, his *turning water into Wine*, and his *feeding thousands* with a *little food* —— But he that will examine *Transubstantiation* as afore-described, shall find it to have more that is *contrary to nature*, than all these, by far. The substance of the dead body of Christ or *Lazarus* did not vanish; but remained to be the *organized Recipient matter* of the re-entring soul. There were *no Accidents without substances*, or other such things as are mentioned before. The multiplying of food, could at the most be but a *new Creation* ; But it was *real food*, and none of the contradictions or absurdities before recited. The turning of *Water into Wine* was *likest this* in the Papists opinion ; but indeed little like it. For the *matter* of the

water

water there remained, with the *form of Wine*, and so became the *Matter of Wine*, and did *not vanish*: And here was *real Wine*, and *real substance*, and *not Accidents without substances, deceiving all the senses or Intellectual perceptions.* The same may be said of the miracles of the Apostles, compared with Transubstantiation.

2. And as to the *Number*, though Christs and his Apostles Miracles were *very many*, yet there is no Scripture-evidence that they were for number comparable (for so much time) to *every Priests.* Christs miracles are set down in the sacred history in *such order*, and the Evangelists so much agree in reciting the *same miracles*, that (though St. *John* say) the *world could not contain the Books that should be written*—— yet we find no probability that they were neer so common as *Masses* are: when in several places where Christ came, they that looked after Miracles and Signs were denyed them, and had none, but were put off to the *sign* of the *Prophet Jonah*, &c. Yea *Herod* and *Pilate* were in this denyed their *desired satisfaction*; and they that call to him for a miracle on the Cross. And so of the Apostles. But every Priest doth his miracles *as oft as there is a Mass*, though *every day.*

3. And as to the *Facility* I said before, that [*in his own Country*, among his *own kindred, he could do no mighty work save that he layed his hands on a few sick folk and healed them*, and *he marvelled at their unbelief*] Mark 6. 4, 5, 6. And he some time *groaned in spirit, and wept*, (as for *Lazarus*). And the Disciples *could not cast out a Devil*, Mar. 9. 18, 28. Luk. 9. 40. It was not to be done *but by fasting and prayer.* Its like *Paul* would have cured *Trophimus* if he could, when *he left him sick.* And as holy men spake, not when, nor as they pleased, but *when and as they were inspired by the*

Holy Ghost: so did they *work miracles*, not arbitrarily, but at such times and in such manner as the spirit moved them.

But any the most wicked Priest can do it *at his pleasure, any hour of the day*: and that but by reciting *Hoc est corpus meum*. Many other disparities appear in what is said before.

IV. The *End* of the Gift of Miracles confuteth the feigned Miracles of Transubstantiation. The *End* of Christs gift was to prove him to be *of God* (as is aforeshewed) and to prove his *Apostles to be of God*, and to confirm the *Gospel* which they Preached, *Mar.* 16. 17, 18, 19, 20. *Heb.* 2. 4. As the gift of Tongues so other wonders, were to *convince unbelievers*, 1 Cor. 14. Act. 2. & 4. 30. & 5. 12. & 7. 36. & 8. 13. & 14. 3. 2 Cor. 12. 12.

But the miracles of Transubstantiation are known to *no unbeliever*; nor to any one in the world by any sense; and have no *such End*, but a contrary effect.

The Apostles who were to convert the world, and next Christ, to do the greatest good, were therefore to do the *greatest miracles*: And it was their argument for Christ, Joh. 7. 31. *When Christ cometh will he do more miracles* than *these which this man hath done?* Yet now every ignorant Priest pretendeth to far more, who doth but tempt Infidels to deride Christianity by the pretence; as we do Mahometanism, for *Mahomets* sport pretended with the Moon, and other such delirations.

V. God is not to be said to work Miracles and cross the established course of nature without proof. But these pretended Miracles have no proof—— No man living perceiveth them by sense. And that God telleth us of no such things by supernatural Revelation, shall be further shewed anon: In the mean time, it may satisfie

us,

us, that they *bring* us no proof, but their own affirmation, which they require us to believe.

VI. The *Matter* of these pretended Miracles is expresly contradicted by the Word of God, as shall be proved in the next Chapter.

VII. *Ad hominem*; Do not the Papists forget themselves here, and contradict their other suppositions?

So they do by forbidding to eat Flesh in *Lent*: And yet say they eat Christs flesh in *Lent*: When *Ireneus* cited by *Oecumenius Com. in* 1 *Pet. c.* 3. bringeth in *Blandina* proving to the Heathens that Christians did not eat flesh and drink blood in the Eucharist, because that they use even to abstain for exercise sake, from Lawful flesh.

1. They make Miracles to be one evidence of *sanctity*, and therefore *Canonize* men, when they think that they have proof that they wrought Miracles: And yet maintain that a Whoremonger, Drunkard or Heretick may do many more.

2. They make Miracles a proof that they are the *true Church*, and say that among *us* there are *no Miracles*; and yet they confess that every Priest, *among us* and all others, whom they account Schismaticks and Hereticks, do more Miracles than *Christ did*; if they consecrate frequently.

3. They burn men to ashes for *working miracles*, even for *making God*; if so be, they do it not in the Roman fashion.

4. They confess that the *other Sacraments* are not thus made up of Miracles; no not *Baptism*, which is our *Christening*, and washeth us from our sins: And yet *this Sacrament alone*, must by a multitude of Miracles differ from the rest.

4. Whether the Doctrine of their St. *Thomas* and his followers and others, that the *formal words of this Sacrament have a created effective virtue by which they instrumentally make the change* (3. q. 78. a. 4. c.) be not an absurdity rather than a proper miracle. For

words Physically move but the *air* first, and the *terminus* of the *aires motion* (*e.g.* the *ear*) next : and next that, if it be an intellectual, or other animal recipient, the sense, and *fantasie* next, and so on : But the *Bread* and *Wine* have no *sense* nor *fantasie* nor *Intellect* : And to say that the *moved aire* is the means of turning them into the body and blood of Christ, is still to multiply miracles.

5. Do they not too much magnifie the *common work* (and consequently the *office*) of a *Priest*, above the work of a *Pope* or *Prelate*, who seldom consecrate ? when the Priest worketh so many Miracles more than they ?

6. They conclude that a sinner that hath *Voluntatem peccandi* receiveth Baptism in vain, as to its ends of pardoning him, and therefore should not receive it (*Concil. Rom. Epist. Gregor. 7. Aquin. 3. q. 68. a. 4. c. &c.*) And yet, be the sinner never such an hypocrite or Infidel, he eateth Christs real flesh nevertheless, yea against his will, if he do but the outward act.

7. Is it not strange that an *Infidel* receiveth as verily the real flesh and blood of Christ as a *Saint*, and yet not the *benefits* or *effects* ? As if Christs flesh and blood could be in a mans body without his benefit : When he hath promised that *he that eateth him, shall live by him.* Yet see the measures of their faith and Church : Saith *Aquinas* (*3. q. 80. a. 3. ad 2.*) [*Unless perhaps an Infidel intend to Receive that which the Church giveth, though he have not true faith about other Articles or about this Sacrament*] then he may receive sacramentally.

CHAP.

CHAP. VI.

The fourth Argument. This Miraculous Transubstantiation is expresly contrary to the Word of God, in Scripture.

Arg. 4. THe Papists say that there is no bread after the words of Consecration: Gods word saith, There is *Bread* after the Consecration: Therefore the Papists speak contrary to the Word of God.

I. In 1 *Cor.* 11. It is called expresly BREAD after consecration no less than three times in three verses together, 26, 27, 28. [" *For as oft as ye eat this Bread* " *and Drink this cup, ye shew the Lords death till he* " *come. Wherefore whosoever shall eat this Bread and* " *drink this cup of the Lord unworthily shall be guilty of* " *the Body and blood of the Lord. But let a man exa-* " *mine himself, and so let him eat of that Bread and drink of that Cup*]: Here they that call for *express words of Scripture* for our doctrine, without our consequences, may see their own faith expresly contradicted, and our opposition justified: The Holy Ghost here *expresly* calleth it *Bread:* And yet no expresness nor evidence will satisfie them.

P, By *Bread* is meant that which *was Bread* before, or else that which *nourisheth* the soul as *Bread* doth the body: And so it is metonymically only called *Bread*, as Christs Flesh is called *Bread* in *Joh.* 6.

R. Why then do you call for *express* texts of Scripture as our proof, when that *expresness* signifieth nothing with you; but you can say, It is a *metonymie* or a *metaphor* at your pleasure, But you say so against notorious Evidence: The Apostle calleth it *Bread* so often over and over, as if he had foreseen your inhumane heresie : He calleth it *The Bread which is to be Eaten*, joyned with *Drinking* the *Cup* ; never once calling either of them the *Flesh* or *Blood* of *Christ*, but as he reciteth Christs words which he expoundeth. Yea he telleth us that *eating this bread*, and *drinking this cup*, is *to shew the Lords death till he come* ; where he calleth us to look back at *Christs death* as past, in our *Commemoration*, and to *look forward* to his *personal coming* as *future* ; but never telleth us that we must kill Christ and eat him our selves (when we have *made him*), nor that his body is there present under the accidents of Bread and Wine.

But the rest of the Scriptures as expresly justifie our doctrine. 1 Cor. 10. 15. *The Cup of blessing which we bless, is it not the Communion* (or *Communication*) *of the blood of Christ* : And *the Bread which we break*, *is it not the communion* (or *participation*) *of the body of Christ* ?] Here it is the *Cup* and the *Bread* after Consecration, if the Holy Ghost may be believed.

And in the next words the Apostle repeateth it in his reason [*For we being Many* are *One Bread*, and *One Body* ; *For we all partake of one Bread* (or Loaf).] Is not here express proof ?

So *Act*. 20. 7. When we came together to *break Bread* ——— And *v*. 11. He *ascending*, and *breaking bread*, and *eating* &c. Here it is twice more called *Bread* after the *Consecration* (which ever went before the *Breaking*).

So *Act*. 2. 42, 46. It is twice more called *Breaking of Bread*.

And what else can the recitation of Christs institution mean, 1 Cor. 11. 23, 24. *Panem accepisse*, . *fregisse* ; to have *taken Bread*, and *having given thanks*, *to have broken* ? What is it that he *brake* ? Its non-sence if it

have

have no accusative case that it respects? And plain Grammatical construction tells us then, that it must be that before mentioned, What he *Took* he *blessed*, and *brake* and *gave*: But he *took Bread* and the *Cup*. The same is in *Mat.* 26, 26, 27. and the other Evangelists.

II. The Scriptures expresly (*Act.* 2, *&c.*) make the *Killing of Christ*, and *drawing* his *blood*, to be the heynous sin of the Jews, for which some Repented and others were cast off: Therefore it is not to be believed that Christ did first *kill* or *tear himself*, and *shed his own blood*; or that his disciples did kill him, or tear his flesh and shed his blood, before the Jews did it. And if they tore his flesh and drank his blood, and yet killed him not, the event altered not the fact: The Jews did but *break his flesh* and *shed his blood*. If you fly to a *good intention*, *Paul* will come in for some further excuse for his persecution.

III. 1 Cor. 10. 21. *Ye cannot drink the cup of the Lord, and the cup of Devils: Ye cannot be partakers of the Lords table* and of *the table of Devils.* — Here note 1. That the same phrase is used of the *Participation* of the *Lords* mysteries and the *Devils*. But it was not the *flesh and blood* or the *substance* of *Devils* which the Idolaters ever intended to partake of: but only their *sacrifices*.

2. It is here called only the *Table* and the *Cup*, and not the *flesh* and the *blood*.

3. It is said that They *could not partake of both*: whereas according to the Papists doctrine, if a man should partake of the *Idols sacrifice* in the morning, and of the *Lords Table* in the evening (without repentance,) he should *really partake of Christs own flesh and blood*; which the Text saith cannot be done.

P. It meaneth only, You *cannot Lawfully*, or you

 ought

ought not to partake of both, but not that it is *impossible* or never done.

R. No doubt but it meaneth that They *ought not*, or *cannot Lawfully*; but thats not all: The text plainly meaneth, *You cannot* have *communion with both:* You may take the *bread and wine* at your peril; but you cannot partake of it as a *sacramental feast* which God prepareth you, and so partake of *Christ* therein.

And the same is said (expounding this) 2 Cor. 6. 15. *What concord hath Christ with Belial ——— and what agreement hath the temple of God with Idols?*] Intimating that Communion with God and Idols, Christ and *Belial*, are (so far) inconsistent: But by the Papists doctrine an Idolater and Son of *Belial* may partake of the very *substance of Christs body* and *blood*, into his *body*, as verily as he partaketh of his meat and drink.

IV. The Scripture teacheth us expresly to judge of sensible things by sense. Luk. 24. 39. [*Behold my hands and my feet, that it is I my self: handle me, and see; for a spirit hath not flesh and bones as ye see me have.* And *when he had thus spoken, he shewed them his hands and his feet.*] And v. 43, [*he did eat before them*] to confirm their faith. But they could have no more sensible evidence of any of this, than we have of the being of *Bread and Wine*, or some sensible substance after Consecration. Joh. 2. 9. *they tasted the water turned into Wine*, and were convinced.

P. But the *Body* of Christ here is not a sensible thing.

R. But *Bread* and *Wine* are sensible things.

P. But *They are not There*; and so are no objects of sense.

R. But all our senses say that *They* are *there*; and by them we must judge.

P. Your *senses* perceive nothing but *Accidents*: and your *understanding must believe God*, and so (as you noted

noted out of *Aquinas* before) there is no deceit either of sense or Intellect.

R. Though this be answered fully before, I will again tell you, That these two notorious falshoods are all that you have to say against *Humanity* in this case, thats worth the noting. I. It is false that you say that *sense perceiveth* not *substance:* When I take up a staff or stone in my hand, I do not only feel Roughness or Smoothness, *&c.* but a *substance:* It is a *quantitative*, and *qualitative substance*, which I feel, taste, smell, see and hear: And this I perceive by *sensation* it self, as the medium to the Intellect. It is not the *sense* indeed, but the *Intellect* that giveth it the *Logical notion* or *definition* of a *substance*; but it is the *sense it self* that by *sensation perceiveth it*; and to deny this is to deny all sense.

And if it *were not* so, How could any *such substance* be *known?* when it cannot come into the Intellect but by the sense?

II. ☞ Your great cheat (or errour) is by confounding the first and *natural-necessary perception* of a *sensibile sensatum* or *incomplex object*, by the *Intellect*, with the *second conception* of the *Names* of *things*, or of Organical second notions, and the *third conception* of them Artificially by the use of these names and Organical notions, and the fourth perception of Consequents from those conceptions. To know by *Believing* is but the third or fourth sort of knowledge, and presupposeth the two first. If a man had never heard a *name* or *word* in his life; yet by *sensation* as soon as he saw, smelt, tasted, heard, handled things, his *Intellect* would have had a *perception* of the *Thing it self* as it was sensate; And this is the *Intellects first perception:* And this is it which falleth under our question, *Whether the Intellect in this first perception of a substance* or *Thing as sensate, be deceived or not*, when the Thing hath the Conditions of of an object before mentioned. 2. Next this we learn or invent *Names* and *organical notions* for things: And whether these be *true* or *false*, and whether they be *apt* or *inept* is all one. This is but an arbitrary work of art. 3. Next this we conceive of things by the *Means* of these *Names* and *second notions*, and examine the *Congruence:* and so we define them: And this is but a work of *Artificial Reasoning*, and presupposeth the first *Natural necessary* perception. Now *Faith* belongeth partly to *this*, and partly to the *fourth*, which is The raising of Conclusions, and the weaving of methods; and presupposeth the first, yea and the second: It is but an assent given by the means of an Extrinsick Testimony of God, that this particular *Word* is *True*, *&c.* Now if the Intellect in its *first Perception* (*natural and necessary*) of the *Thing it self*, as *sensate*, be deceived, if *faith* should be contrary to it, 1. It must be such a *Faith* which is the *immediate contrary perception of a sensate object*; which is *no faith*, nor is any such possible, (properly called faith): 2. And if faith can come after and undeceive the Intellect, by saying that God saith otherwise, yet this would be no *prevention* of *its deception*, but *a cure*, presupposing the said deception as the disease to be cured. So that to say as *Aquinas* that faith *preventeth the deceit of the Intellect*, is a falshood contrary to the nature of man, and his natural way of acting, as he is composed of soul and body.

I have said this over again, lest errour get advantage by the brevity and unobservedness of that which I said before.

CHAP.

CHAP. VII.

Argum. 5. *All these miracles have not the least proof; yea, the Scriptures fully direct us to a cross interpretation of the Papists pretended proofs; which also are renounced by themselves.*

I Know of no Scripture proof in the World that the Papists pretend to, but the words, *This is my Body*, and *This is my Blood*, and such like. And that these are no proof I shall fully prove to any impartial man.

I. The very *nature* of the *Sacrament* instituted by Christ with his expressed *End*, command our Reason to expound the word [is] of *signification*, representation or exhibition, and the word [Body] and [Blood] of a new *Relative form* only, that is, of a *body and blood Representative*, (which is all one in effect): As a piece of Gold, Silver, or Brass, is by the law and stamp turned really into the *Kings Current Coine*; and so hath a new *Relative form*: so that you may truly say that there is a change made of the Gold, or Silver into the Kings Coyn: and it is no more to be called *meer Gold* or *Silver* (though it be *Gold* and *Silver* still), because the *form denominateth*, and the new form is now that in question which must denominate. Or as a Prince that is marryed in *effigie* or by a *Representative* to a woman, is not there personally; and yet it is aptly said, *This is the Prince which is betrothed* or *marryed to thee*. Or as we say of Pictures, *This is* Peter, *or* Paul, *or* John. Or as when we deliver a man possession of a

House

House by a Key, or *of Land by a twig and a turf*, or of a *Church* by the *belrope*, &c. and say, *Take, this is such a House*, or *such a piece of Land*, or *Church*, &c. As this is ordinary intelligible speech among all men, so Christ tells them that he would be so understood.

1. In that his *Real natural body spake this*, of the *Bread and Wine* which was *not* his natural body: His real natural body was present, visible, entire, unwounded, his blood unspilt, and did eat and drink (the *other*, as the Papists hold, as being the same): And can any living man imagine that the Disciples who understood not his Death, Resurrection, Ascension, &c. yet understood by these four words, when they saw Christs body alive and present, that this Bread and Wine was that same Body and Blood, without any more questioning?

2. In that he bids them, *Do this in Remembrance of him*; which plainly speaketh a commemorating sign: Who will say at his last farewell when he is parting with his friends, *I will stay among you*, or *keep me among you*, in *Remembrance* of me? So for Christ to say, *Eat me in remembrance of me*, were strange.

II. It may put all out of Controversie to find, that Christs *words* of *one half of the Sacrament are* (as they confess) *figurative*; therefore the *other* must be so judged also. Luk. 22. 20. This *Cup is the new Testament in my blood, which is shed for you*: 1 Cor. 11. 25. [*This Cup is the new Testament in my blood.*] And here no man denyeth a double Trope at least: no man expoundeth it, that the *Cup* or the *Wine was the New Testament it self*. And yet it is as expresly said, as it is that the *Bread* is the *Body* it self. How then will they prove that one is spoken properly, and the other figuratively?

III, There

III. There is no more found in these words to assert Bread to be Christs Body, than is found in a multitude of such phrases in Scripture asserting things which ...men expound otherwise. As in Joh. 15. 1. *I am the ...ne and my Father is the husbandman* : Joh. 10. 7, 9. *...m the door*—— Joh. 10. 14. *I am the good Shepherd ...d know my Sheep* : Psal. 22. 6. *I am a worm and no ...n* (which being a prophesie of Christ, a Heretick imi...ing you, might deny Christs humanity :) 1 Cor. 10. 4. *...at Rock was Christ*—— 1 Cor. 12. 27. *Ye are the ...ly of Christ* — Mat. 5. 13, 14. *Ye are the Salt of the ...th : Ye are the lights of the World*—— Joh. 6. 63. *...e words that I speak unto you they are spirit and ...y are Life.* Abundance such are in the Scripture, as ... flesh is grass : Christ is the Lamb of God : the Lyon ... the Tribe of *Juda* ; the bright Morning Star ; the ...d Corner Stone, *&c.*

And it is yet more fully satisfactory, that the Hebrew ...stantly putteth [*is*] for [*signifieth*] as you may ...d in all the old Testament ; having no other word so ... to express [*signifying*] by : And as Christ spake ...er that manner, so the New Testament ordinarily imi...eth ; As *Daniel* and the *Revelation* agree in saying, ... the Visions, *This is* such or such a thing, instead of *...e signifieth* it. So Christ, *Matth.* 13. 21, 22, ..., 37, 38, 39. He that soweth *is* the Son of man : ... field is the world : the good seed are the ...ildren of the Kingdom ; the tares are the children of ... wicked one : the enemy is the Devil, the Harvest ... the end. The reapers are the Angels—— And ...is ordinarily.

IV. Yea, the same kind of phrase used before ... the Passeover, teacheth us how to expound this : ...od. 12. 11. *Ye shall eat it in haste, It is the Lords*

Passeover ——

Passcover—— verſ. 27. *It is the ſacrifice of the Lords Paſſeover.*

V. Yea the *ordinary way* and *phraſe* of *Chriſts teaching* may yet farther put us out of doubt. For he uſually taught by Parables, and expreſſeth his ſenſe by ſuch aſſertions: As Matth. 13. 3. *Behold a ſower went out to ſow*, &c. Luk. 15. 11, 12. *A certain man had two ſons, and the younger ſaid*, &c. Luk. 12. 16. *The ground of a certain Rich man*, &c. Luk. 16. 19. *There was a certain Rich man*, &c. Mat. 21. 28. *A certain man had two ſons*, &c. Verſ. 33. *There was a certain houſholder which planted a Vineyard*, &c. The Goſpel aboundeth with ſuch inſtances, which teach us how to interpret theſe words of Chriſt.

VI. But moſt certainly all thoſe forementioned texts teach it us, which expreſly call it *Bread after the Conſecration.* If we will not believe the Holy Ghoſt himſelf, who ſo frequently calleth it *bread*, it is in vain to alledge any text of Scripture in the Controverſie.

Now to feign a courſe of *ordinary Miracles*, *Greater* and *more* than Chriſts, and this to *every Prieſt*, how ignorant and impious ſoever; to pretend that every Pope and Biſhop can for money ſell the Holy Ghoſt or the Gift of Miracles, in Ordination; and all this when no eye ſeeth the Miracles, when it is confeſſed that Angels cannot *naturally ſee it*, yea when all mens ſenſes perceive the contrary; and all this becauſe, that Chriſt ſaid *This is my Body*, while abundance ſuch ſayings in Scripture, yea the words about the *Cup it ſelf*, are confeſſed to be tropical, and when the Scripture expreſly telleth us that there is *Bread.* Judge whether it be poſſible for Satan to have put a greater ſcorn upon the Chriſtian faith, or a greater ſcandal before the enemies of it, or a greater hinderance

to

to the Worlds Conversion, than to tell them, you must renounce not only your Humanity but all common sense, if you will be Christians, and be saved, or suffered to enjoy your estates and lives.

VII. Lastly, It is ordinary with their subtilest Schoolmen to confess that this their doctrine of Transubstantiation cannot be proved from Scripture, and that they believe it only because their *Church saith it*, which must be believed, and because that by the same *Spirit* which wrote the Scripture, the *Church is taught* thus to expound it. So that all their faith of this is by them resolved into a phanatick pretence of *Inspiration*; As I have elsewhere shewed out of *Durandus*, *Paludanus*, *Scotus*, *Ockam*, *Quodl.* 6. *li.* 5. *q.* 31. *Rada vol.* 4. *Cont.* 7. *a.* 1. *pag.* 164, 165.

And no General Council ever determined it till that at *Rome* under *Innoc.* 3. Where saith *Matth. Paris*, many decrees were proposed or brought in by the Pope which some liked and some disliked. And this was 1215 years after Christs birth. And *Stephanus Æduensis* is the first in whom the name of Transubstantiation is found, about the year 1100.

CHAP.

CHAP. VIII.

Arg. 6. *From the Nature of a Sacrament.*

Arg. 6. THat Doctrine which by consequence denyeth the Lords Supper to be a true Sacrament, is false.

The Papists doctrine of Transubstantiation by consequence denyeth the Lords Supper to be a true Sacrament: Therefore the Papists doctrine of Transubstantiation is false.

The *Major* I know no man that will deny that we have now to deal with.

The *Minor* needeth no other proof, than the common definition of a Sacrament, and Christs own description of this Sacrament in the Scripture.

I. *Aquinas* concludeth 3. *q.* 60. *a.* 1. that a *Sacrament* is a *sign*; and *a.* 2. that it is a sign of a thing sacred as it sanctifieth men; and *a.* 3. that it is a Rememorative sign of Christs passion, a demonstrative sign of Gods Grace, and a prognosticating sign of future Glory: And *a.* 4. that it must be *Res sensibilis* a *sensible thing*, it being natural to man to come to the knowledge of things intelligible by things sensible, and the Sacrament signifieth to man spiritual and intelligible Goods: and *a.* 5. that they must be things of Divine determination, *&c.*

But, 1. If the Bread and Wine be gone, there is nothing left to be a *sign*, a Real sensible sign, to lead us to the knowledge of spiritual and intelligible things. If they say that the *species* of *Bread* and *Wine* is the *sensible sign*, what mean they by that cheating word

[*species*?]

[*species?*] Not the *specifying form* or matter, but only the *outward appearance*. And is it a *true* or a *false* appearance? If True, then there is Bread and Wine: If *false*, it is a false sign: And what is that false appearance which God maketh a Sacrament of? It is plainly nothing but the Accidents of *Bread* and *Wine* without the substance. But, 1. When they take the Cup from the Laity, and deny them half the Sacrament, sure there are then no *Accidents of Wine*. Is there either Quantity, Colour, Smell, Taste, *&c.* of *Wine?* They will not say it. So that here is no *sensible sign* as to one half.

2. And herein they deal far more inhumanely with us than the Infidels themselves: For when they plead against Christ and Scripture, they grant that the *common principles* and *Notitiæ*, which all mankind acknowledge, are the *certain unquestionable light of Nature*. But the Papists deny not only the *Notitias communes*, but *common sense*. It is nothing with them to damn all the world, that will not believe contradictions. They say that the *Quantity* of *Nothing* endued with the *Qualities*, the *Actions*, the *Passion*, the *Relations*, the *quando*, *ubi*, *situs* of *nothing*, is the Sacramental *sign*. Inhumane contradiction! 1. *Gassendus* and others say truly, that an *Accident* is not properly *Res*, but *Modus Rei*, (*vel Qualitas*, as he calleth it.) 2. *Quantity* doth not Really differ a *re quanta*: and to say, [*The Length, Breadth, Profundity of Nothing*] is a notorious contradiction: And so it is of the other Accidents. There is no *Real sensible sign*, and therefore no Sacrament, where there is *nothing*, but the *quantity*, *colour*, *taste*, *smell*, *&c.* of Nothing.

See my *More Reasons for the Christian Religion*, and the Lord *Herbert de Veritate*.

3. And they cannot, they dare not say, that Christs

Real Flesh and Blood, is the *Sacramental sign*: For, 1. It is not *sensible*; 2. It should be then the *sign of it self*: The sign and the thing signified cannot be the same.

II. The very *substantiality* or *corporeity* of the *Bread* and *Wine as such*, is part of the *sign*: As Christ saith, *Behold and handle me, a spirit hath not flesh and blood, as ye see me have*: So he taketh *Corporeal bread and wine* in their sight, and *breaketh it*, and *poureth it out*, and *giveth it them* to see, to feel, to taste, to eat, that they may know it is *true bread and wine*, the signs of his True Body and Blood. So that to deny the *Corporeity* is to deny *Christs Corporeity* in *its signs*; and tendeth to the old Heresie of them that held that Christ had but a *phantastical body*, or was not indeed Crucified, but seemed so to be: They teach Hereticks to argue, *The sign was no Real substance: Therefore neither the thing signified.*

III. The *nutritive use* of the *bread* and *wine* was another part of the *sign*, as all confess: As *bread* and *wine* are the *Nutriment* of the body and life of man, so is Christ *crucified meritoriously*, and Christ *glorified efficiently*, the life of the soul. And he that denyeth the *Nutritive sign*, denyeth the *Sacrament*: But it is not the *false appearance*, or *phantasm*, or *accidents* of *bread* and *wine*, that are the natural *nourishers* of man: Therefore he that denyeth the *nourishing substance*, denyeth the *Real sensible Sacramental sign*.

Saith *Bellarmin de Euchar. l.* 3. *c.* 23. [*In the Eucharist we receive not corporal food that the flesh may be thence nourished and made fat: but only to signifie inward refection.*] So that he acknowledgeth this to be part of the Sacramental sign. So *Gregor. Valent.* saith that [*The chief and essential signification of this Sacrament is that which by external nourishment is signified*

signified, the internal spiritual refection of the soul by the body of Christ.] So that denying the *nourishing sign* is destroying the essence of the Sacrament.

IV. The *breaking of the Bread* and *pouring out the Wine* is confessedly another part of the Sacramental sensible sign. But, 1. When there is no *Wine*, there is no *pouring it out*: 2. And if there be no *Bread* neither, there is no *breaking it*: Can that be *broken* which is not? They that deny (as the Papists do) that the *Bread* is *broken* (saying that only the *Quantity of Nothing* is broken) deny the sensible Sacramental sign.

And here I may note, that we do not well to contend with them for denying the Cup only to the Laity, and granting them only the Bread, when indeed they grant neither, but deny them both: There is (say they) no more *Bread* than *Wine*, but only a false appearance of it.

V. Lastly, The Apostle 1 *Cor.* 10. 16, 17. sheweth that one Sacramental use of the Bread was to signifie the *Unity of Christians*, who are *one Bread*, and *one Body*, as *one Loaf* is made of many *Corns*. But that cannot be *One*, which is *Nothing*: *Ens*, *Unum* & *Verum convertuntur*. To say with *Greg. Valent.* and *Bellarmine*, that because it *was Once bread*, and *one bread*, therefore the accidents of it remaining now signifie that we are *one bread*; is but to say, that There was once a fit sign, but then there wanted the form: Now after Consecration, there is no Sacramental sign, but yet there is a Sacramental form: And in what *Matter* is that form? Doubtless it can be no where but in the Brain or Mind of man: That is, man can Remember that once he saw Bread: This is the *species* of *bread* in his Intellect: This *species* is the *sign*: And so we have found out another sense of the *species of bread*, than many think on; viz. It is that which is called *The spe-*

cies intentionalis, or the *Idea* or conception of *bread* in a *mans fantasie* and *mind*: And so indeed the Sacrament is with them an *invisible thing*: for it is only in mens minds: There is no Sacrament on the *Altar*, but in the *thoughts*: And so who hath a Sacrament, and who not, we know not: And a man may by *thinking* make a Sacrament when he will.

CHAP. IX.

Of the Novelty of Transubstantiation.

R. I Once thought to have next proved out of the Current of Antiquity, the Novelty of this inhumane doctrine of the Papists, and that the Antients commonly confessed, that there was true *Bread* and *Wine* remaining in the Sacrament after Consecration: But, 1. I should but *tempt* and *weary* ordinary Readers, who neither *need* any such arguments (having *Sense* and *Scripture* to give them satisfaction) nor are able to try them: For it is an indirect kind of dealing, to expect that the unlearned, or those that are strangers to the Writings of the Antients, should believe this or that to be their mind and sayings, meerly because I tell them so. And if they read the plainest words, they know not whether I rightly recite them, but by believing me. And it is as unreasonable on the other side, that the Papists should expect, either by their Citations or their general Affirmations, that the Readers should believe them, that the Antients were for Transubstantiation. Till men can both read the Authors themselves, and try the Copies, they can have no sure historical notice what the Fathers held, except by the

the common consent of credible Reporters or Historians: Not while one side saith, they say this, and the other side saith they say the contrary, and yet their Books are to be seen by all. We may bid them *believe us*, and the Papists may bid them *believe them*, and a Priest may cheat them by saying, that his word is the Churches: But though this will produce a humane belief in the Hearers or Readers, as by advantages it is most taking with them, yet that fallible belief is all the Certainty that it can afford them. Therefore I think it most ingenuous and reasonable to give men such arguments as they are capable of understanding and improving to certain satisfaction.

2. Because they that can study such Authors as have gathered the sentences of the Antients in this Controversie, may find it so fully done by *Edmund. Albertinus* in his second Book, that they can need no more.

P. You know that *Albertinus* is answered.

R. And I know that he is again Defended: And who doubteth but you can answer me copiously, if I did maintain that the Sun giveth light: What is it that a man cannot talk for? especially they that can hope to perswade all the Christian world, that they must be damned, unless they will believe that all mens senses are deceived, and that God is the great Deceiver of the world.

P. But how can you think to please God and be saved, if you be not of the same faith as the Church hath alwayes been of? All the antient Fathers and Catholick Church were for Transubstantiation; and are you wiser and in a safer way than they?

R. You have lost your credit with me so far, as that your word is no oracle to me: If I must not believe my *own* nor *other mens senses*, I am not bound to believe *you*: at least when I know you speak falsly.

 But

But I pray tell me, How know you that the Church and Fathers did so believe?

P. Because the present Church saith so; which cannot err.

R. Do not your own Writers say, that a General Council and Pope may err in matter of fact? and that they did so in Condemning Pope *Honorius* and in other Cases?

P. Yes: but this is a matter of faith.

R. Is it not a matter of fact, what this or that man said, and what doctrine the Church at such a time did teach and hold?

But how know you that the present Church doth say so, that this was the faith of the antient Church?

P. By their testimony in a General Council.

R. Did you hear the Council say so?

P. No: but the Church telleth me that the Council said so.

R. Who is it that you now call the Church which tells you so?

P. My Superiours, who have it from the Pope, and their Fathers.

R. Are your Superiours that told you so, the Church? Or is the Pope the Church? If so, What need you say a Council is the Church? And how know you that the Pope and your Superiours err not in a matter of fact?

P. I know it by the Decrees of the Council yet extant.

R. 1. But if *sense* be deceitful, how know you that you ever read such Decrees? 2. How know you that they are not forgeries, or since corrupted?

P. The Church is a safe keeper of it's own Records.

R. Still

R. Still what mean you by the Church? The Vulgar neither keep nor underſtand your Councils. The Council of *Trent* is long ceaſed: No other General Council hath been ſince, to tell you what are the true Decrees of that Council. The Pope is not the Church: And he may err in a matter of fact: What then is the Church that tells you certainly what the Council of *Trent* decreed? Tell me if you can.

P. We have ſuch common hiſtorical Evidence and Tradition, as you have for your Acts of Parliament when the Parliament is ended. The preſent Governours preſerve them.

R. Very good: It is the Office of the Governours to take that Care, but therein they are not indefectible and infallible; but *they* and the *publiſhed Laws*, and the *notice of the whole Land*, and the *Judicial proceedings* by them in the *Courts of Judicature* make up a *Certain Hiſtorical Evidence*. And ſo it may be in your Caſe: And when you have talkt your utmoſt, you can ſhew no more. And have not *we* the ſame Writings of Fathers and Councils as *you* have? You dare not deny it. Why then may not *we* know what is in them as well as *you?* And I pray you tell me, Whether your Antiquaries, ſuch as *Albaſpinæus*, *Sixtus Senenſis*, *Petavius*, *Sirmondus*, *&c.* do prove what *Cyprian*, *Optatus*, *Auguſtine*, *&c.* held, by the judgement of the Pope or Councils, or by citing the words of the Authors themſelves? And do *Crab*, *Binnius*, *Surius*, *Caranza*, *&c.* prove what one Council ſaid by the authority of *another*, or by the *Records* themſelves, yet viſible to all?

P. Thoſe Records themſelves, even the viſible Writings of the Fathers and Councils are for Tranſubſtantiation.

R. Till you have perſwaded me out of my ſenſes, I will not believe you. I pray you tell me if you can of any Author or Council that ever used the name [Transubstantiation] before *Stephanus Æduensis* after the year 1100, *de Sacram. Altar. c.* 13.

P. Though the name be new, the Doctrine is not.

R. Tell me next, what *General Council* did ever determine it, before the Council of *Laterane* under *Innoc.* 3. *an.* 1215.

P. Not expresly: for General Councils need not mention it, till the *Albigenses* Hereticks gave them occasion by denying it.

R. Was it an Article of faith before? If it were, either the Councils are not the measure of your faith, or it is very mutable.

P. Among all your questionings answer me this question if you can. If that General Council decreed Transubstantiation, what could move them so to do, if it were not the faith of the Church before? Were they not all of the same mind the day before they did it? and so the day before that, and the day before that, &c. Or do you think that they were against Transubstantiation the night before, and awaked all of another mind the next morning? What could make all the Pastors of the Church think that this was the true faith, if they did not think it was the antient faith? And what could make them think it the antient faith, if it were not so? Did not they know what their Fathers held? And did not their Fathers know what their Fathers held? The same I say of the Council of *Trent* also.

R. Thus men that must not believe the common sense of mankind, can believe the dreaming conjectures of their brains, and sit in a corner, and thence tell the world what can and what cannot be done by publick assemblies, at many hundred years and miles distance. Who would not laugh at a Fryer, that in his Ceil would tell by moral conjectures, all the thoughts and motions of an Army

or

or Navy, that never ſaw them, and contrary to the experience of thoſe that were on the ground and intereſſed in their Councils and actions. Obſerve how many falſe ſuppoſitions go to make up your cheats.

1. You ſuppoſe this a true *General Council*, which is a pack of factious Prelates ſubject to the Pope, and aſſembled at *Rome* in his own Palace, under the awe of his preſence and power. And as if the ſmall number after at *Trent* had ſpake the minds of all the Churches.

2. You ſuppoſe *all the members* of a *Council* to be of *one mind*: when as they determine by the *Major Vote*. And oft times the difference is not above *two* or *three*, and its poſſible *one Voice* may turn the ſcales: And perhaps *one*, or *two*, or *ten* may be abſent one day, and preſent another, and ſo the Cry of [*the Judgement of all the Biſhops in the world*] may ſignifie no more, but that *two or three* of the other ſide ſtaid a little too long at dinner that day, while the other party carryed it by their abſence. And I pray you where hath God promiſed, that the faith of an hundred and one ſhall not fail, when the faith of ninety nine of the ſame company may fail (ſuppoſing the Council to be two hundred): Or why are the one hundred and one the Biſhops of all the world, and not the ninety nine?

3. Do you think we never read the Hiſtory of the Council of *Trent*? and before them, of the Councils of *Ariminum*, *Epheſ.* 2, yea, *Calcedon*, *&c.*? And yet muſt we ſuppoſe, that men come thither all of one mind? when they have ſuch ſhameful Contentions? Such cunning contrivances to get the majority of Votes? Such awe and terror from the power of the Chief? and ſuch carnal dependances and reſpects to their ſeveral worldly intereſts? Yea, ſometimes fighting it out unto blood (as *Dioſcorus* and *Flavianus* caſe doth ſhamefully evince?)

4. And

4. And must we suppose mens minds to be *changed in their sleep*, when the *awe* or the *oratory* of other men change them? Do we not know the Course of the *Parliaments* of *England* of later times? How much a few men of more than ordinary parts and interest, can do with the rest? And how oft the major Vote hath gone against the sense of the far greater number of the House?

5. And do we not know, that ordinarily he that is sent to the Council from a Province, is chosen as it pleaseth the Pope, the King, or the Archbishop, or some in greatest power; and rarely according to the free-will and sense of the greater part of the Clergy. If five hundred to one of the Clergy of a Kingdom be of one mind, and the Prince, or chief men, or powerfullest Prelates be of another, they will send a Bishop thither of their own mind.

6. Do you think we know not that all the Papists are not past the third or fourth part of the Christian world? Why then should their sense be called the sense of all the Christian world?

7. Do you think we know not how little reason you have to say, that the Council at *Laterane* spake the sense of all the Church? When the Decrees were but proposed by Pope *Innocent*, and recited there without any due Synodical deliberation, and some liked them, and some disliked them? as you may find in *Math. Paris* in *K. John*, *Nauclerus Gener.* 41. *ad an.* 1215. *Godefridus ad an.* 1215. *Platina in Vita Innoc.* 3. And this one of your late false Scriblers in a Book for Toleration also saith; Though the Disputers against Dr. *Gunning* and Dr. *Pierson* copiously and confidently justifie that Council: and indeed with you it passeth for an Approved one.

8. And

8. And were not your arguing as strong for the Council of *Ephes*. 2. and that at *Arim*. and *Sirmium*, and divers at *Constantinople* disallowed, and those at *Constance* and *Basil*, (where were many times the number of the Council at *Trent*)? Did these Councils all go to bed of one mind, and rise of another? Or did they not know what their Fathers faith was? Why then do you reprobate them, and deny that which they decreed as of faith? Is it not a shame, to talk of [*the Bishops of all the world*] and [*Tradition from their Fathers*] when your meaning is but that *All these may err*, and do *oft err*, unless *one man*, the *Pope* approve them? But where *sense* is renounced, we must not expect *modesty*.

P. But the antient Councils and Fathers are against you, as is to be seen.

R. It is utterly false: I will not abuse the Reader so as to carry him into a Wood, and lose him among a multitude of old Books, when he hath more satisfactory evidence enough at hand.

But, I. As to all your Citations from true antiquity (for your forged Authors and corrupted Testimonies we regard not) they are answered by this one true observation, that when old Writers sometimes say, that after consecration it is [*No more bread and wine, but the body and blood of Christ*], their whole Context plainly sheweth, that they mean that it is no more *MEER* or *Common Bread* and *Wine*; and usually they so speak. Because *forma denominat*, and it is the *ultimate form* that denominateth, all antecedent forms being but the *dispositio materiæ*. As if the question be, *Whether a Shilling be Silver or Money?* Before the Coining, it was *but Silver*; but after, it is no more *Common Silver*, but *Money*: *Silver* is but the *matter*, and not the denominating form, Is your Garment to be called *Cloth*, or or a *Cloak?* Before the making it was but *Cloth*, but now it is not meer *Cloth*, but a *Cloak*, The ſame I may ſay of the Kings Crown and Scepter, or of any *Relative*, *Repreſentative* or *Perſonating form* that is added to any matter or man. This is the plain meaning of the Antients.

II. And as to what they ſay againſt you, I will now only give you a few brief inſtances.

1. *Juſtin Martyr. in Dial. cum Tryph.* ſaith, [*The offering of Flower delivered to be offered for them that were cleanſed of the Leproſie, was a Type of the BREAD of the Euchariſt which our Lord Jeſus Chriſt commanded us to make in remembrance of his paſſion*, &c.]

And more plainly *Apolog.* 2. (indeed the firſt) [*When the Preſident hath given thanks, and all the people acclaimed, thoſe that with us are called Deacons, diſtribute to every one preſent BREAD and WINE and Water, and bring them to thoſe that are abſent.*]

2. *Irenæus* ſaith *lib.* 4. *c.* 34. [*For as the Bread which is of the Earth receiving the divine invocation, is not now Common Bread, but the Euchariſt, conſiſting of two things, the Terrene and the Celeſtial*, &c.]

See more out of him in *Albertinus*, at large.

3. *Tertullian cont. Marcion l.* 3. *c.* 19. [*Calling Bread his Body, that hence you may underſtand that he gave to Bread the Figure of his body.*]

And before *l.* 1. [*He reprobated not ——— Bread, by which he Repreſenteth his very Body.*]

And *lib.* 4. *cap.* 40. [*The Bread which he took and diſtributed to his Diſciples he made his body, ſaying, This is my Body; that is, The figure of my body. —— And what he would have Bread then ſignifie, he ſufficiently declared, calling Bread his Body.*]

And

And it is a notable paſſage of *Tertullians* againſt the Academicks that queſtioned ſenſe, *lib. de anim. c.* 17. [*What doſt thou, O procacious Academick? Thou overthroweſt the whole ſtate of life: Thou diſturbeſt the whole order of nature; Thou blindeſt the providence of God himſelf; as if he had made mens lying and deceitful ſenſes to be the Lords, in underſtanding, honouring, diſpenſing and enjoying all his works: Is not the whole Condition* (of man) *ſubadminiſtred by theſe.*] And after [*We may not call thoſe ſenſes into queſtion, leſt Chriſt himſelf muſt deliberate of their certainty* (or muſt diſtruſt them). *Leſt it may be ſaid, that he falſly ſaw Satan caſt down from Heaven, or falſly heard the voyce of his Father teſtifying of him; or was deceived when he touched* Peters *Wives Mother* —— *or perceived not a true taſte of the Wine which he Conſecrated in the memorial of his blood.*] Many ſuch places are in *Tertullian.*

4. *Origen* is large and plain to the ſame purpoſe in *Matth.* 25. calling it [*Bread* and a *Typical and Symbolical Body, which profiteth none but the worthy receivers, and that according to the proportion of their faith, and which no wicked man doth eat,* &c.] Many more ſuch places *Albertinus* vindicateth.

5. *Cyprians* Epiſtle to *Magnus* is too large this way to be recited. As [*Even the Sacrifices of the Lord declare the Chriſtian Unanimity, connexed by firm and inſeparable love: For when the Lord calleth Bread his body* (*or his body bread*) *made up of many united grains,* &c. *And when he calleth the Wine his Blood,* &c.] So *Epiſt. ad Cæcil.*

6. *Euſebius Cæſar. demonſtr. Evang. l.* 1. *c.* 10. [*Celebrating daily the memorial of the body and blood of Chriſt*] —— [*Seeing then we receive the memorial of this Sacrifice to be perfected on the Table, by the ſym-*

bols

bols of his body and most precious blood——] And *l.* 8. [*He delivered to us to use, Bread as the symbol of his own body.*]

7. *Athanasius's* words are recited by *Albertinus l.* 2. *p.* 400, 401, *&c.*

8. *Basil. de Spir. Sanct.* saith, [*Which of the Saints hath left us in Writing the words of invocation, when the Bread of the Eucharist, and the Cup of blessing are shewed?*]

9. *Ephrem (in Biblioth. Photii p.* 415. *Edit. August.)* saith, [*The body of Christ, which believers receive, loseth not his sensible substance, and is not separated from the intelligible grace.*]

And *ad eos qui filii Dei,* &c. [*Take notice diligently how taking Bread in his hands, he blessed it, and brake it, for a figure of his immaculate body, and he blessed the Cup and gave it to his Disciples as a figure of his pretious blood.*]

10. *Cyrillus (vel. Johan.) Hierosol. Catech. Mystag.* calls the *bread* indeed *Christs body,* but fully expounds himself *de Chrysmate, Cat.* 3. *pag.* 235. [*For as the Bread of the Eucharist, after the invocation of the Holy Ghost, is no more Common Bread, but is the Body of Christ: So also this Holy Oyntment is no more meer Oyntment, nor (if any one had rather so speak) common, now it is consecrated; but it is a Gift* (or Grace) *which causeth the presence of Christ and the Holy Ghost; that is, of his Divinity.*] As the *Oyntment* is Grace, or the *Holy Ghost,* just so the *Bread* is the *body of Christ,* as he saith after *Cat.* 4. It is not only what we see *(* Bread and Wine *)* but more.

11. *Hierom cont. Jovinian. l.* 2. *The Lord as a type (or figure) of his blood, offered not water but wine.*

12. *Ambrose de Sacram. l.* 4. *c.* 4. [*This therefore we assert, How that which is Bread, can yet be the body*

of

of Christ.]——— And [*If Christs speech had so much force, that it made that begin to be which was not, how much more is it operative, that the things that were, both Be, and be changed into something else.*] And [*As thou hast drunk the similitude of death, so thou drinkest the similitude of pretious blood.*]

13. *Theodoret in Dialog. Immutab.* dealeth with an Eutychian Heretick, who defended his Error by pleading that the *bread* in the Eucharist was changed into the body of Christ: To whom saith *Theodoret*, [*The Lord who hath called that meat and bread which is naturally his Body, and who again called himself a Vine, did honour the visible signs with the appellation of his body and blood; not having changed their Nature, but added Grace to Nature.*]

And in *Dialog. 2. In confus.* he saith, [*The divine Mysteries are signs of the true body.*] And again, answering the Eutychians pretence of a change he saith, [*By the net which thou hast made, art thou taken.* ☞ *For even after the Consecration, the Mystical signs change not their nature: For they remain in all their first SUBSTANCE, figure and form, and are Visible, and to be Handled as before. But they are understood to be the things which they were made, and are believed and venerated as made that which they are believed to be.*] Would you have plainer words?

14. *Gelasius cont. Nest. & Eutych.* saith, [*Verily the Sacraments of the body and blood of Christ which we take, is a Divine thing, for which and by which we are made partakers of the divine nature.* ☞ *And yet it ceaseth not to be the Substance and Nature of Bread and Wine. And certainly the Image and similitude of the body and blood of Christ are celebrated in the action of the Mysteries.*] What can be plainer?

15. *Cyril. Alexandr. in John* 4. *cap.* 14. saith, [*He gave to his believing disciples fragments of Bread, saying, Take, Eat, This is my body.*]

16. *Facundus lib.* 9. *cap.* 5. *pag.* 404. (as cited by *P. Molin. de Novitate Papismi*) [*We call that the body and blood of Christ which is the Sacrament of his body, in the consecrated Bread and Cup.* ☞ *Not that the Bread is properly his body, and the Cup his blood; but because they contain the Mysterie of his body and blood.*]

But I am so weary of these needless Transcriptions, that I will trouble my self and the Reader with no more. *Albertinus* will give him enow more who desireth them: And no doubt but with a wet finger they can blot out all these, and teach us to deny the *sense of words*, as well as our senses.

D. But you said also, that the *Present Church and its Tradition is against Transubstantiation, as well as the Antient:* How prove you that?

R. Just as I prove that the Protestants are against it.

By the *present Church*, I mean the far greater part of all the Christians in the world. The Greeks with the Muscovites, the Armenians, the Syrians, the Copties, the Abassines, and the Protestants, and all the rest who make up about twice or thrice as many as the Papists.

That they hold that there is *true Bread and Wine after Consecration*, all impartial Historians testifie, both Papists and Protestants, and their own several Coun-

opick Liturgy about the *Real presence.*) But I need no more proof of that which no faithful History doth deny.

And then I need not prove, that Transubstantiation is against the most General or Common Tradition. For all these Christians, the Greeks, Armenians, Abassines, &c. profess to follow the Religion which they have received from their Ancestors, as well as the Papists do: And if the Papists be to be believed in saying that this is the Religion which they received from their forefathers, Why are not the other to be believed in the same case? And if the Popish Tradition seem regardable to them, Why should not the Tradition of twice or thrice as many Christians be more regardable? And if in *Councils*, the Major Vote must carry it; Why not in the Judgement and Tradition of the Real body of Christs Church? As for their trick of excepting against them as Schismaticks and Hereticks, to invalidate their Votes and Judgement, we despise it, as knowing that so any Usurper that would make himself the sole Judge, may say by all the rest of the world: But as they judge of others, they are justly judged by others themselves.

CHAP. X.

The second part of the Controversie, Whether it be Christs very Flesh and Blood into which the Bread and Wine are Transubstantiated.

R. OUr first Question was, *Whether there be any Bread and Wine left after Consecration*; Our second is, *Whether Christs Real Flesh and Blood be there, as that into which the Bread and Wine are changed?*

And herein 1. I do freely grant, that the change of Christs Body by Glorification is so great, as that it may be called, though not a Spirit, yet a *Spiritual body*, as *Paul*, 1 *Cor.* 15. saith *Ours* when Glorified shall be; that is, A body very like in purity, simplicity, and activity to a Spirit: And the general difference between a spirit and body was not held by many of the Greek Fathers as it is by us: And if the second Council of *Nice* was Infallible, no Angel or other Creature is *Incorporeal*: Or as *Damasus* saith, [They are Corporeal in respect to God, but Incorporeal in respect to gross bodies.] The perfect knowledge of the difference between *Corpus* and *Spiritus*, except by the *formal Virtues*, is unknown to mortal men.

2. I grant therefore, that our senses are no Competent Judges, *Whether Christs true body be in the Sacrament?* no more than Whether an Angel be in this room? There are bodies which are Invisible.

3. I grant that it is unknown to us, how far Christs Glorified body may extend? Whether the same may be

to confute them that ſay, *Light* is a *Body* ; nor them that ſay, It is a *ſpirit* : nor them that ſay, It is *quid medium* as a *nexus* of both : I mean *Æther* or *Ignis*, viſible in its Light. And it is an incomprehenſible wonder, if *Lumen* be a real *radiant* or *Emanant* part of the Sun, that it ſhould indiviſibly fill all the ſpace thence to this earth, and how much further little do we know. So for the extenſions of Chriſts body, let thoſe that underſtand it diſpute for me.

4. And I will grant that it is very probable that as in Heaven we ſhall have both a *Soul* and *Body*, ſo the *Body* is not like to have ſo near an *Intuition* and *fruition* of God as the *ſoul*. And whether the Glorified *Body* of *Chriſt* will not be there a *medium* of Gods Communication of Glory to our *bodies*, yea and his *glorified ſoul* to our *ſouls*, as the Sun is now to our eyes, I do not well underſtand : only I know that it is his prayer and will, that *we be with him where he is to behold his Glory* ; and that *God and the Lamb will be the Light of the Heavenly* Jeruſalem.

5. And I am fully ſatisfied that it is not the ſigns only, but the *Real Body and Blood* of Chriſt, which are given us in the Sacraments (both Baptiſm and the Euchariſt) : But *how given us? Relatively, de jure* ; as a man is Given to a Woman in Marriage ; or as a houſe and land are delivered to me, to be mine for my uſe ; though I touch them not. Thus 1. A *right* to *Chriſt* is given us : 2. And the *fruits* or *benefits* of his *Crucified body* and ſhed blood, are *actually* given us, that is, *Pardon* and the *Spirit*, merited for us thereby.

6. And among the Benefits given us, beſides the Relative, there are ſome ſuch as we call *Real* or *Phyſical terminatively*, and *hyperphyſical originally ut à Cauſa*, which are the *ſpirit of Holineſs*, or the *Quickening*, *Illuminating* and *Sanctifying* influence of the ſpirit of

Chriſt upon our ſouls. And the Sacrament is appointed as a ſpecial means of communicating this.

7. I have met with ſome of late who ſay, that Indeed Chriſts Body and Blood in his humbled ſtate, were not really eaten and drunk by the diſciples, at his laſt ſupper: For the *fleſh* profiteth not to ſuch a *uſe*: But that his *Glorified Body* is *ſpiritual*, and is extenſively communicated, and inviſibly preſent under the form of Bread in the Sacrament; and that as we have a *Body*, a *ſenſitive life*, and an *Intellectual ſoul*, ſo Chriſt is the life of all theſe reſpectively; *viz.* His *Body* is made the *ſpiritual nouriſhment of our Bodies*; his *ſenſitive ſoul* (for which the word *Blood* is put, becauſe it is in the blood in animals) is the food or life of our ſenſitive ſouls; and his Intellectual *ſoul*, of ours: And to theſe uſes they aſſert the *Real preſence* and *oral* participation of Chriſts Glorified body.

To all which I ſay, 1. Whether or how far an inviſible ſpiritual Body is *preſent*, ſenſe is no judge; nor can we know any further than Gods word telleth us. 2. That Chriſt in his Glorified *ſoul* and *Body* is our Interceſſour with God, through whom we have all things, we muſt not doubt. 3. That Chriſt in his Humane and Divine Nature now in Heaven, is that Teacher who hath left us a certain word, and that King who hath left us a perfect Law of Life, whom we muſt obey, and a promiſe which we muſt truſt, we muſt not queſtion. 4. That the Holy Ghoſt who is our ſpiritual Life, is given us *by*, *from* and *for* Chriſt our Mediator, we muſt take for certain truth.

themselves, and not in their effects only they were thus communicated to us, I understand not, either by any just conception of the thing it self, or any proof of it from the word of God. But if any can help me to see it, I shall not refuse instruction.

Nor can I see why the *soul* of Christ should be said to be given in the *Wine only*, and not in the *Bread*; Nor why by this kind of Communication he may not as truly be said to be given us in other Ordinances as in the Eucharist: Nor know I what they mean by the *Forms* of *bread* and *wine*, under which they say that Christs Body and blood is given: But I am past doubt that *Bread* and *Wine* are still really in substance there.

And whereas the same men say that It is Christs humbled flesh and blood as sacrificed on the Cross that is *Commemorated*, but his *Glorified Body* and *soul* only which are *Communicated* and *Received*, I must say, 1. That Christ plainly tells us of his *Giving us his Sacrificed Body* or *flesh* it self to eat, as he is the *Lamb of God that taketh away the sins of the World*: And he saith, *Take, Eat, this is my Body which is broken for you*, &c. so that the same body is Commemorated and Communicated: But *how Communicated?* In the *effects* of his sacrifice: His *Body* was given a *sacrifice* to God *for us*, and the *fruits* of that sacrifice *given to us*. And thus he was given a sacrifice for the *life of the world*; And thus we do receive him: By our bodily taking and eating the Bread, we profess that our souls take him to be our Saviour and Cause of our Life, *both* as *Purchasing* and *Meriting* it on Earth, and *Interceding* and *Communicating* it in and from Heaven.

2. And this Doctrine will not serve the Papists turn, who tell us that *Bread* and *Wine* are ceased, and that

ſubſtance of the bread and wine are turned; and that his natural Body before his death, was in the ſame ſort given under the forms of Bread and Wine as now; and will not be beholden to this ſubterfuge.

And indeed it is ſtrange if the Sacrament at the *firſt Inſtitution* ſhould be *One thing*, and ever after another thing; and that the *Bread* ſhould ever ſince be turned into *Chriſts body*, upon the Prieſts Conſecration, and not be turned into it, (becauſe not yet glorified) upon his own words [*This is my Body.*] Therefore we muſt let this go, and ſpeak of what they own and hold indeed. And as for any other *Bodily preſence, influence* or *communication* of Chriſts *Body* or *Soul*, beſides that which they call Tranſubſtantiation, we have nothing to do with it in this Controverſie.

That the ſubſtance of the *Bread* and *Wine* is not turned into the ſubſtance of the *fleſh* and *blood* of Chriſt, is proved.

I. Becauſe the Glorified *Body* of *Chriſt* is *not formally* and *properly Fleſh and Blood*: Though it be the ſame *Body* which was *Fleſh* and *Blood*. The Apoſtle *Paul* ſaith, 1 Cor. 15. 50, 51. [*Now this I ſay, brethren, that fleſh and blood cannot inherit the Kingdom of God, nor doth corruption inherit incorruption; Behold, I ſhew you a myſterie: We ſhall not all ſleep, but we ſhall all be changed.*] It is not only Dr. *Hammond*, but other of the beſt expoſitors who ſhew that by *Fleſh* and *blood* and *corruption* here is not meant *ſin*, but *fleſh* and *blood formally conſidered*; which is ever corruptible: And the Papiſts commonly confeſs this. If therefore it be *fleſh* and *blood* which the *bread* and *wine* are turned into, then either Chriſt hath two bodies, or two parts of one, which are utterly heterogeneal, one *fleſh* and *blood*, and the other not; one corruptible and the other incorruptible.

II. And this feigneth Chriſt to be *often Incarnate*,

even thousands and millions of times; And to lay down that Incarnate body again as oft as it corrupteth, and to take up a new one as oft as the Priest please; and yet all but one. Whereas the Church and Scripture have ever told us but of *one Incarnation* of Jesus Christ.

III. And it is expresly contrary to his promise Joh. 6.51. *I am the living bread which came down from heaven: If any man eat of this bread, he shall live for ever: And the bread which I give is my flesh which I will give for the life of the world* —— v. 34. *Who so eateth my flesh and drinketh my blood hath eternal life* ——— *He that eateth my flesh and drinketh my blood, dwelleth in me and I in him. As the living Father hath sent me, and I live by the Father, so he that Eateth me, even he shall live by me* —— *He that eateth of this bread shall live for ever* ——.] These are the express promises of Christ. But the Papists say that *wicked men* and *unbelievers eat the flesh of Christ*, who shall not *live for ever*, nor have *eternal life*, nor *dwell* in *Christ*, but are more miserable by their hypocrisie.

I pass by abundance of other arguments, because commonly used, and these are as many as my ends require; and I would make the Reader no more work than needs.

CHAP. XI.

The Conclusion of the first Book: The Causes of Popery.

R. I Have now made plain to you, 1. *What the Protestants Religion is,* (or at least *my own*, and all that I perswade you or any other to embrace.) 2. And also that it is granted to be all true by the generality of the Papists (as is explained and proved.) 3. And I have told you, by an enumeration of some particulars, why I am not a Papist, and why I do disswade you from it. 4. And I have made good my first *charge*, in the point of Transubstantiation, if any thing in the world can be proved. The second I shall leave till another time, *viz*. To shew you how far their Religion (as Popish) is from Infallible Certainty; and what horrid confusion is among them; and how they have done much to promote Infidelity in the world, by building Religion upon some notorious untruths, and upon a multitude of utter uncertainties. Though I doubt not but among them there are many true Christians, who practically resolve their faith into the surer evidences of Divine Revelation, yet I shall clearly prove to you, that all those whose practical faith is no surer or better, than the notional opinions of their Divines will allow, have no certain faith or Religion at all: And what impudency is it to make men believe, that there is no *certainty* of Religion to be had, but in their way, who build their Religion upon such a multitude of *uncertainties* and certain falshoods, as will amaze you when I come to open them to you, *viz*. that ever so

many

And if I be not by death or other greater work prevented, I hope in order to make good all the rest of the Charges before mentioned, which are our Reasons against the Popish way of Religion. In the mean time tell me what you think of that which is already said.

D. I know not how to confute what you have said: And yet when I hear them on the other side, me thinks their tale seems fair, and I cannot answer them neither: so that between you both, we that are unlearned are in a sad case, who must thus be tost up and down by the disputations of disagreeing Priests, so that we know not what a man may say is certain.

R. To this I have several things to say; 1. *Ordination* doth not make men *wise*, *holy*, *humble* and *self-denying*; but sets such men apart for the sacred office, who seek it, and have tolerable gifts of utterance: And it is too ordinary for worldly minded men, to make a worldly trade of the Priesthood, meerly for *ease*, and *wealth*, and *honour*. In which case, do you not think that the Papists who have multitudes of rich benefices, prelacies, preferments, and Church-power, and worldly honour, are liker to be drawn by worldly interest, than such as I that am exceeding glad and thankful, if I might but preach for nothing?

2. Do you lay your faith and salvation upon plausible discourses? and will you be of that mans faith, whom you cannot confute? Then you must be of *every mans* faith: or indeed of *no mans*. There are none of all these sects, so hardly confuted, as a *Porphyry*, a *Julian* or such like *Infidels* who dispute against *Christ*, and the *truth of the Scriptures*? or such Sadducees as dispute against the *Immortality of the soul*. Alas, the rattle of Papists, Pelagians, Antinomians, Separatists, Quakers, and

these than with a Papist or any other Sectary, you would shake the head, to hear one man dispute for an universal Monarch, and another dispute against a form of prayer, and another whether it be lawful to Communicate with dissenters, *&c.* while so few of them all can defend their foundations, even the *souls Immortality* and the *Scriptures*, nor confute a subtle Infidel or Sadducee.

3. What if we *all agreed* to say that there is no Bread in the Sacrament after Consecration? Were it ever the truer for that? Will you be deceived as oft as men can but *agree* to deceive you? There is a far greater party Agreed against Jesus Christ (even five parts of the World) than that which is agreed for him: Will you therefore be against Christ too? There are more Agreed for *Mahomet* (a gross upstart deceiver) than are agreed for Christ: And doth that make it certain that they are in the right?

4. Will you deny all your senses, and the senses of all the World, as oft as you cannot answer him that denyeth them? Upon these terms, what end will there be of any Controversie, or what evidence shall ever satisfie man? Have Papists any surer and more satisfying evidence for you, than sense?

I pray you tell me; Did you ever meet with any of them that doubt of *another life*, or of the *Immortality* of the soul?

D. Yes, many a one: I would we were all more certain than we are.

R. And

D. They ſay that our talk of Prophets and ſupernatural revelation are all uncertainties; and if they could ſee, they would believe. Could they *ſee* ſuch *Miracles* as they read of: Had they ſeen *Lazarus* raiſed, or Chriſt riſen from the dead, *&c.* Had they ſeen Angels or Devils or Spirits appearing: Had they ſeen Heaven or Hell, they would believe.

R. And are not you more obſtinate than they, if you will not believe that there is any *Bread* and *Wine*, when you *ſee*, *feel*, *ſmell*, and *taſte* it, and all men that have ſenſes are of the ſame mind? What is left to ſatisfie you, if you give ſo little credit to the common ſenſe of all the world?

D. But I oft think that the *faith* of all *the Church* is much ſurer than my ſenſe, or my private faith: At leaſt it is ſafeſt to venture in the common road, and to ſpeed as the Church ſpeedeth, which Chriſt died for, and is his Spouſe.

R. 1. But do you think that the opinion of the Papal faction who are not the third part of the Univerſal Church, that is, the Chriſtian world, is the *faith of all the Church?* Why call you *Opinion faith?* and a ſect and faction, *All the Church?*

2. Indeed if all the Church did ſet their *ſenſes* againſt mine, I would rather believe them than my ſenſes: For I ſhould think, that I were in that point diſtracted, or my ſenſes by ſome diſeaſe perverted, which I did not perceive: I mean if it were in a caſe where they had the affirmative: As if all *England* ſhould witneſs that they ſaw it Light at Midnight, I would think my eyes had ſome impediment which I knew not of, if I ſaw none. But this is not your caſe; The Papiſts themſelves do not ſet all their *ſenſes* againſt yours:

not say, that [*We and all men, except the Protestants, do see, and feel, and taste that There is no Bread and Wine.*] But contrarily, You have *the senses of all the world*, and the *faith* of two or three parts of the Christian world, against the Opinion of one Sect, which Schismatically call themselves All the Church.

D. But suppose that they err in this one point, they may for all that be in the right in all the rest: Who is it that hath no error? I must not for this one forsake them.

R. 1. I will stand to their *own judgements* in this, Whether all their foundation and faith be not uncertain, if any one Article of their faith prove false? They are all (that ever I knew) agreed of the affirmative: And will give you no thanks for such a defence.

2. And if we come to that work, I shall prove all the rest of their opinions before mentioned to be also false.

D. What then if I find but one point false in the Protestants Religion? Must I therefore forsake it all as false?

R. 1. Still remember to distinguish between our *Objective* and our *Subjective faith*: or if you understand not those words, between *Gods Revelation* and *Mans Belief* of it: or the *Divine Rule* and *Matter* of our faith, and our *faith* it self. And about our own *Belief* you must distinguish between a mans *Profession* of *Belief*, and the *Reality* of his belief.

All true Protestants *profess* to take Gods *word alone*, or his Revelation in *Nature* and *Scripture*, for the whole *Matter* of their Divine Belief and Religion. But who it is that *sincerely believeth* little do I know: nor how *much* of this *word* any singular person understandeth, and believeth, I can give you no account of.

If

o were that which we dispute of, I would for no mans but mine own. In this e as many *Faiths* and *Religions* as *men* : hath his *Own Faith* and *Religion* : And it a man erreth in one point, it followerreth in another. They that believed *ection was past*, believed a falshood : believed that *Christ was the Messiah* : t thought it lawful *to eat things offered* t they erred not in *believing in Christ*. the world, its like, have the same del faith and knowledge; as I oft said beour professed *object* of *faith*, that is, e false, in *one thing*, we could not be true in any thing.

old you before, 1. That a man may be t *one part* of Scripture is *Gods word*, than se some *Copies* are doubtful in the dif some particular *words* or *sentences*; hem that so differ is Gods word, we oft so much as we are sure is the word of re is true : So if the Authority of some nce doubted of, (as 2 *Pet. Jam. Jud.* yet be by any, it followeth not that they uth of any, which they know to be the 2. Or if any do hold that the Penmen their natural fallibility in some by-histances or words, it would not follow, of the *Gospel* or *Christian faith* is doubtlainly as the Kernel of it, delivered in all nd also by infallible Universal Traditiin the *Sacrament, Creed, Lords Prayer*

And

And our case also much differeth fro this: For We profess that our *objectin* word) is *Infallible*, and *we* are *Infallib.* *believe it:* But we confess that we ar *understand* some parts of it; and so far being imperfect: But the Papists say, th. *Councils* and Universal-*Practicers* are p *lible*, so as not to be lyable to any misu any Article of faith (say some) or Arti *faith* (say others): And so they make of *Believing* to be Commensurate and with Gods *word of faith*; and therefor to question them in all, if they err in on to a gift of never erring in any.

D. But is it not a great reason tc them rather than to you, when *They* *Infallibility*, and You confess that you a your *Belief?*

R. This is to be the subject of our ne and therefore not now to be anticipated; you, that It is a meer noise of ambiguc ceive the heedless that cannot search out them. 1. We not only *Pretend*, but *P* *that our Christian Religion* is altogether which end I have written divers Tre. 2. And we profess that all the mystical C (that is all sincere Christians) do trul *believe* all that is *Essential to Christianit* of the *Integrals* as they can know. 3. *that the* *Catholick Church-Visible* (that *sors of Christianity in the world*) do *p* *Essentials* of *Christianity*, and are *I* *profession.*

But we hold withall, that there is

Church, or *Biſhop*, no *Synod* or *Council*, that is *ſo Infallible*, but that, 1. They that hold to the *Eſſentials* may miſunderſtand and err about ſome *Integrals*: 2. And thoſe *perſons* have no Certainty that they ſhall not *err* by Hereſie or Apoſtacy from the Eſſentials themſelves: So that the *Church* is *Infallible*, because it is *eſſentiated* by *believing an Infallible Word*; which who ever believeth not, ceaſeth to be of the *Church*: not *Gods Word infallible*, becauſe the *Church* or any *number* of men *believe* it, or ſay Its true: For *Truth* is before *Knowledge* and *Faith*: As *Ariſtotle* was a Philoſopher, becauſe he underſtood and taught the doctrine of real Philoſophy; and not that doctrine called *Phyſicks* or Philoſophy, becauſe that *Ariſtotle* knew or taught it.

But, alas, What work ſhall I ſhew you when I come to open their bewildring uncertainties?

D. But to deal freely with you, methinks their way of meaſuring out the *Neceſſaries* in Faith and Religion according to mens various parts and opportunities, ſeemeth to me more ſatisfactory than yours, who fix upon certain points (as the *Baptiſmal Covenant*) as *Eſſentials*. For there is great diverſity of mens Capacities.

R. This cometh from confounding ſeveral Queſtions as if they were all one.

1. It is one Queſtion, *What is the Chriſtian Religion?*

2. ☞ It is another Queſtion, Whether the Chriſtian Religion be abſolutely neceſſary to the ſalvation of all thoſe to whom it was never competently revealed?

3. And it is another Queſtion, Whether more than the Eſſentials of Chriſtian Religion be not neceſſary

to

to the ſalvation of many who have opportunity to know more? Alas, what work doth Confuſion make in the world!

To the firſt, It is evident that as Mahometaniſm is a thing which may be defined, ſo much more may *Chriſtianity*: Who that writeth of the ſeveral Religions of the world, Ethnick, Jewiſh, Mahometan, and Chriſtian, do not take them to be diſtinguiſhable and *diſcernable?* Eſpecially when Chriſt hath ſummed up *Chriſtianity* into a *Covenant*, and given it us in expreſs words, and affixed a flat promiſe of ſalvation to the true *Covenanters*, and the Church hath ever called our Baptiſm, our *Chriſtening?* Is Chriſtianity Nothing? If Something, Why may it not be defined, and differenced from all falſe Religions? And if ſo, It hath its Eſſential Conſtitutive parts. All this is plain to Children that will ſee.

2. And then as to the ſecond queſtion, it concerneth not our Controverſie at all. It is but Whether any Infidels may be ſaved? Or any that are no Chriſtians? And if it could be proved, that any are ſaved that are no Chriſtians, do you thereby prove that they are *Chriſtians*, or members of the Chriſtian Church? or that Chriſtianity is not a Religion which may be defined?

3. And as to the third queſtion, We are on all ſides agreed in it, That they that have more than the *naked Eſſentials* of Chriſtianity revealed to them aptly, are bound to believe more: Yea, it is hardly conceiveable that any one ſhould know and believe the Eſſentials only, and no more: It is not Eſſential to the Chriſtian Covenant or Chriſtianity to know that the Name of Chriſts Mother was *Mary*; or that *Pontius Pilate* was the man that condemned him; And if

an

an Ignorant man thought that his continuance in the Grave was four dayes, I do not think that this would damn his soul to Hell: (Much less the not believing that *Mary* dyed a Virgin.) And yet it is not like that any man should come to the Essentials of Christianity by any such way, as should acquaint him with no one of these, or any point besides the said Essentials.

And yet it is certain for all this, that he that *truly receiveth* the *Essentials*, and is *true to the Baptismal Covenant, shall be saved*, whatsoever else he want: But it is as true, that he that *Receiveth the Essentials, will* (from the same *principles* and *obligations*) receive *more*, when it is aptly notified to him:. And he that truly Covenanteth, will honestly keep the Covenant he maketh; which bindeth him still to learn of Christ. But if any man be saved without the *Essentials*, he must be saved without Christianity.

D. But you know that they distinguish of faith *Explicite* and *Implicite*: He may be *Implicitely* a Christian that believeth not the Essentials *Explicitely*; as long as he believeth that which would infer them, if they were made known to him to be indeed the Word of God.

R. Thus do *Words* abuse and cheat the ignorant: Could you but read their own Dr. *Holden* before cited in his *Analys. fid.* you would find this distinction justly rendred by him shameful and ridiculous, according to their common sense and use of it; and the truer sense delivered and vindicated. An *Implicite faith* or *Knowledge* we confess to be true, as it is opposed to 1. A *distinct*, or 2. To a *well-expressed* faith or Knowledge. For it is *Implicite*, ☞ 1. As to the *Object*, when a *man knoweth the whole matter*, but not

 by

by *distinct parts:* As a man may know a Cup of water, and not know how many drops or drams it is; or he may know a sentence, and not know how many letters are in it. 2. Or it is *Implicite* as to the *Act*, when it is yet but a *crude* imperfect conception, and the *thing* is *really* known, but not the *Logical notions*, or Grammatical names, either the *verba oris* or *mentis* by which it should be expressed: So that the man cannot notifie his knowledge to another. These two are called *Implicite*; the first signifieth *Confused* and *General Knowledge*, and the other *Imperfect* and *undigested*.

Apply this to Mr. *Johnsons* Rejoynder on this Point, and you will see his Vanity.

But to call that *Implicite faith* or *knowledge*, which extendeth only to some *Principles*, and not to the *Conclusions themselves*, is 1. To Call *No-knowledge* and *faith*, by the name of *knowledge* and faith. 2. And by their application to confound the *World* and the *Church*, and to make all the Infidels and Heathens to be Christians, and every Fool a Philosopher.

For, 1. All men of Reason know these two Principles (who own a God), 1. *That God is not a lyer, but all his Word is True.* 2. *That all the Truths in the world are God's, some way or other revealed by him.* Therefore, if they knew that the Gospel were *Gods word*, they would believe it: or if they knew it to be one of those Truths that are in the world, they would take it to be of God. And thus all Infidels, and Turks, and Pagans may (by such abuse) be called *Implicite Christians.*

But why then do the Papists burn the *Protestants*? when if their Religion were true, we are all *Implicitely*

God hath commanded us to adhere to; 5. And that all our Lawful Pastors must be reverenced and submitted to; 6. And all their lawful Precepts obeyed. 7. And all Gods Sacraments holily used; 8. And all Traditions from the Apostles to the Churches received; with many more such: Only we know not that the Pope is our Pastor, or that his Councils are the Church, or have a promise of Infallibility; and so of the rest. And yet we must burn for it, if they can procure it. And yet he is a true believer Implicitely who believeth not the Essentials of Christianity.

But the *Design* which is predominant here is too visible, when this Implicite faith cometh to be described: For it is not a Belief in *God*, or in Christ only that will serve the turn, but it must be a belief in *the Church*, and *their Church*, and their Pope too, or else it will not do. The Implicite faith is the explicite belief of these three Articles: 1. All Gods Word is true: 2. All that is Gods Word, which the Church tells us is Gods Word. 3. The Pope and his Council and Subjects are this Church. And yet this man must be supposed if he know no more, *per impossibile*, not to know that there is a Christ, or who he is as to his Person or Office, or what he hath done, or will do for us: And yet that he hath a *Vicar* and a *Church*. Or else they may know Christ and Christianity before they know that there is any

Pope or Church, and then the Pope hath lost the Game.

D. But if Popery be so senseless a thing as you make it, how come so great a number of persons of all ranks and qualities, Kings, Nobles, Learned men, and Religiously-disposed persons to embrace it? Have not they souls to save or lose as well as you? and do they not lay all their hopes of Heaven upon it? and can such persons, and so many, be so mad and senseless?

R. Do we need thus to ramble round about, as if we would doubt of the *thing* till we know the *Causes* of it? when *we see* and they all confess that they deny all our senses? Will you not believe that there is a Sun, till you know what it is made of? Or whether the Sea ebb and flow, till you *know* the *Causes* of it? I pray you tell me,

Q. 1. Do you think that the Mahometan's is not a very foolish Religion, and their *foundation* (the pretended Mission of their Prophet) without any shew of truth; and his Alcoran (if ever you read it) a heap of Non-sense and Confusion?

D. Yes: I think it deserveth no better thoughts.

R. And do you not know that (though it arose not till about six hundred years after Christ) much more of the world is Mahometan than Christian? And are there not far Greater Emperours and Princes Mahometans than any that are Christians? And have not all these souls to save or lose? And do they not all venture their souls upon that Religion? Why then is not your argument here as good for Mahometanisin as for Popery?

D. Though the Emperours of *Constantinople*, the Great Mogul, the Persian, Tartarian Mahometans,

tans, *&c.* be all Great as to their vast Dominions, yet they are barbarous and unlearned in comparison of the Papists.

R. 1. It is not because they have not as much wit as we: but because they think that our *laborious wordy* kind of learning, is an abuse of wit, and against true Policy, ludicrously or contentiously diverting mens minds and time from those employments which they think more manly and profitable to the Commonwealth; Though no doubt but they do err more unmanly on that extream, But I further ask you,

Q. 2. Do you not think that the Common Religion of the Heathens is very unworthy for any wise man to venture his soul upon? If you have but read how it is described by the Antient Christians, *Justin*, *Athenagoras*, *Origen*, *Arnobius*, *Minutius Fœlix*, *Tertullian*, *Lactantius*, *Eusebius*, *Augustine*, *&c.* you will say that they thought it a ridiculous unmanly Religion.

D. I think no better of it than they did.

R. And 1. Do you not know that almost all the world was then Heathen and Idolaters? Alas, what was *Judæa* (less than *England*) to all the world? Was not the *Roman* Empire, and *Alexanders* before that, far Greater than any Christian Prince hath now? And to this day, are not four sixth parts of the whole world (at least) Heathens and Idolaters? *Brierwoods* Calculation is, that if you divide the world into thirty parts, nineteen are Heathen, six Mahometans, and five only Christians of all sorts: besides the vast unknown parts of the world, which are not like to have any Religion of supernatural Revelation.

2. And do you not know, that *Athens* and *Rome*-Heathen were no Barbarians, but of most polite literature, and the Fathers of the Learning now in use; and that when the Christians arose among them, they accounted them Barbarians? And at this day, and long before us, the *Chinenses* have been addicted to Arts and Literature: And the *Brachmanes* and *Bonzii* are no Barbarians. And have not all these souls to save or lose? And are all these so mad as to cast away their souls upon a senseless contemptible Religion? If your reason be good, how much more will it hold for the Heathens, than the Papists? Alas, what a handful are the Papists in comparison of the present Idolaters! much more in comparison of the *Antient Heathen world*, before *Christianity* and *Mahomitanism* dispossessed them of those parts which they now hold!

With what greater shew of advantage did the Heathens use the Arguments which the Papists do now put their trust in, and lay their Cause upon!

1. Do they talk of *Antiquity*? Why, it was the *Novelty of Christianity* in comparison of Heathenism through the world, which was it that hardned them to contemn and persecute it.

2. Do they talk of *Universality* and *Consent*? Alas, how little a part of the world were the Christians at first, and are the Papists now, in comparison of the Heathens, then and now?

3. Do they talk of Greatness, Empire, Arts and Learning? How little are they as to the first, to the Heathen Empires? And for Learning, they received it of them: And *Aristotle* still is the Schoolmens Oracle. And yet doubtless all these advantages are not sufficient to disprove the follies of Hea-

thenism

nism; nor the badness of their Religion? And yet will so much less serve to support the credit of senseless Popery?

D. But *Christians* may well expect greater helps from God, than Heathens or Mahometans: Therefore that so many Great and Learned and Religious Christians should go such a senseless way to another world, methinks seemeth strange.

R. And are not Greeks, Armenians, Syrians, Abassines and Protestants, all *Christians* as well as they? Their proud schismatical unchristening all but the subjects of the Pope, is a silly proof that we are no Christians, or that they are any better than others; unless Malignity, uncharitableness and Schism be the true Excellency.

1. And are not other Christians *More* than the Papists? Bishop *Bramhall* reckons the Papists to be about the fifth part of Christians: Suppose they be a third part? They are still the *Minor* part.

2. And are not the Protestants as Learned as the Papists? Why then will not your argument hold *against them* as well as *for* them? Have not all these Christians souls to save or lose? And do they not take that for the true Religion on which they trust their souls?

D. But though all these set together are more than the Church of *Rome*, yet no one Sect of them is so great; and what matter is it how many various Sects are?

R. 1. The Greek Church is judged by wise men, to be yet bigger than the Roman, even in this its broken state: But there is no doubt but it was much bigger long after the first division, before the Turk did win the Eastern Empire.

2. But, if it were not ſo, your objection is frivolous. The Queſtion is either of *Different Churches*, or of *Different opinions* and *parties* in the *ſame Church*. As to the firſt, There are but two opinions in the Chriſtian world, that I know of, about the Conſtitution of the *Catholick Church*. The one is the opinion of the *Papiſts only*, ☞ that *The Catholick Church is eſſentially conſtituted* both of *Chriſt, and the Pope* as *his Vicar* and *univerſal Monarch*, with all *his ſubjects*; as the *pars Imperans* and *pars ſubdita*.

The other is the judgement of all other Chriſtians, (that I know or hear of,) that *The Catholick Church* is *eſſentially conſtituted only of Chriſt as the ſupream Head, or King*, or *pars Imperans*, and *his ſubjects* as the *pars ſubdita*; ☞ And that Patriarchs, Archbiſhops, Biſhops, *&c.* are but *Officiales & ſubditi primarii vel nobiles, conſtitutive parts indeed of their particular Churches* (ſome humane, and ſome Divine) but no *eſſential* parts of the *Catholick Church*.

☞ This is the Grand difference between the Papiſts and all other Chriſtians in the World, *What the Catholick Church is? Whether it have any Conſtitutive Univerſal Head* or *Monarch beſides Chriſt?* Now ſeeing that *Greeks, Abaſſines, Armenians* and all agree with us in this againſt the Papiſts, it is evident to them that are willing to ſee that we are all of the ſame *Catholick Church*, though not of the ſame particular Churches, nor all for the ſame Official Miniſters; Becauſe we are all for the ſame Conſtitutive *Head*, and his *ſubjects as ſuch*, and agree in all the Eſſential parts. ☞ So that our differences among all theſe parties or particular Churches or

Coun-

Countries is but the difference of *Opinions* and *parties in one and the ſame Church* ; and not a difference of Catholick Churches (which can be but one.)

And if that be the queſtion, I undertake to prove that there is no one Sect of Chriſtians known under Heaven, that hath ſo many different opinions within it ſelf, (if half ſo many,) nor have written half ſo much againſt one another, as the Papiſts have done.

3. But I muſt not here anticipate my further work: when I come to that, I ſhall ſhew you how *ſmall* and how *diſagreeing* a part of the Chriſtian world the Papiſts are. I have elſewhere recited the words of their *Melchior Canus* who boaſteth, that the Papacy yet ſtandeth, though almoſt all the world, and beſides Princes, almoſt all the Biſhops and Churches have fought againſt it. Was it then the Univerſal Church? And the words of *Reynerius* who ſaith, that the Churches of the *Armenians* and the others planted by the Apoſtles (without the Empire he meaneth) were not under the Pope of *Rome*. I ſhall, if I live to do that work, yet fullier ſhew you, that the Pope was but the chief Patriarch in one Empire, as the Archbiſhop of *Canterbury* is the chief Biſhop in *England* ; and that his General Councils were but General Aſſemblies of the Empire (inconſiderable occaſional accidentals excepted), even as our Convocations, or the Scots General Aſſemblies were, though in a far larger Empire. But all this I have done already in other writings, beyond all reaſonable contradiction.

D. Tell me then, how it cometh to paſs that ſo many Princes, Nobles, Learned men, and Religious can be ſo marvellouſly deluded?

R. Alas

R. Alas poor man; You talk as if you knew not your ſelf nor mankind ! how bad a thing corrupt unſanctified nature is ! Why do you not alſo ask, How cometh it to paſs, that the far greateſt part of the World (even five parts of ſix) are Heathens and Mahometanes ! and that moſt of the World are wilful ſelf-deſtroyers; many ruining their very bodies, Eating, and Drinking, and Whoreing, and Idling them into Gowt, Stone, Dropſies and an hundred Maladies : but far more ruining their ſouls. Why do you not alſo ask, How reaſonable Creatures (of all Profeſſions) are ſo worſe than mad, as to ſell their ſouls and everlaſting hopes, for a dream and ſhadow, or for dirt and dung; even for a few Cups or Morſels, or merry hours, which they know are like the mirth of drunkenneſs, which is quickly gone, and ends in ſickneſs and in ſhame ! For a great Name, and a large attendance in their way to the grave ! For the *thoughts* and *breath* of mortal man ! And for that which all men first or laſt, are forced to call meer *Vanity* and *Vexation !* Were not men mad in ſin, had they never heard a Preacher, the ſight of a dead Carkaſs and a grave would do more to make them ſober and conſiderate, than is done with moſt. When moſt of the World will obſtinately follow the Devil their enemy, by known ſin to everlaſting miſery, againſt all the commands, exhortations, promiſes, threatnings, mercies and warnings of God himſelf, and all the perſwaſions of their trueſt friends, What wonder if the ſame men can be Papiſts or any thing ?

But I will tell you ſome of the particular Cauſes.

I. Abroad

I. Abroad in other Countries, there are all these Reasons easily discernible. 1. Who knoweth not how great an advantage *Education* hath, to form mens judgements to almost any thing, how bad soever? That which children receive, if it be not disagreeable to their sensible interest, how commonly and tenaciously do they follow? Whence is it that the whole Empires and Kingdoms of Pagans are all of one mind; and the Kingdoms of Mahometans of another? One Kingdom almost all Greek Christians and another Papists, and another Lutherans, and another Reformists, *&c*? Hath not education a great hand in this?

2. And the *custome* of the Countrey, and the *company* which they converse with, is of no small power with mens minds. Especially when men live where almost all *are of a mind*, they think that *concord* is a sign of *truth*, and *modesty* forbiddeth them to be wiser than all the Countrey.

3. And when they know few or none of another mind, how should they know what they are? And when they hear an hundred lies against them, and never hear them speak for themselves, they think that the Law of modesty, humanity and converse, oblige them to believe, that so Many, so Great, and so Learned and Religious persons will not impudently lie: When as perhaps the lye it self is a *Tradition* which the lyars received on the same terms in modest credulity from their teachers or fathers.

4. And specially, the Names of *Order*, *Government*, *Unity*, and *Concord*, deceive many millions of souls: For *Order* and *Unity* are justly amiable to nature it self. And the purblind know not an *Image* from a *Man*.

5. Especially

5. Especially when civil Wars, or Church discords have distracted the World, and made men aweary of all that's *present*, and suspicious of all things, which seemed to have a hand in their disappointments; this maketh men hearken to any thing which pretendeth to *certain settlement*, *Order* and *peace*. Even as a man that by turning round is wheelsick, will lay hold on the next post or fixed thing, to keep him from falling down.

6. And when their Teachers make them believe, that all Christians besides them do live like madmen, in Sects and Schismes, distractedly tearing out one anothers throats, What wonder if this make men willing of any way which pretends to peace, and glad to run into any Cottage which will keep them from such a storm?

7. But the great cause is, 1. The *Blindness* of mens minds, 2. The *wickedness* of all unrenewed hearts, and 3. The *power* of *carnal Interest*.

1. Few men are of *great natural parts* for wit, and fewer *improve* them, by any serious study of things spiritual.

2. Almost all men study with the byas of *prejudice* and *partiality*, and as men that *would* have *one side* to be *right*, because it is for their worldly ends.

3. Sin Ruleth in most souls, and the enmity against God and his Laws prevaileth in carnal minds, *Rom.* 8.6, 7, 8. And *enmity* is an ill student and seeker of truth; and friendship is an incompetent judge of sin.

4. None but a few self-denying persons can bear to be reproached as Hereticks and Schismaticks by all about them.

5. Especially

5. Eſpecially the countenance or diſcountenance of *Great ones*, doth more with ſuch than Heaven and Hell.

6. And that's not all, But he that will not be a Papiſt, in moſt of their Countreys muſt be *undone*, and in many muſt be *rackt*, *tormented* and *burnt*: And it is but few that have learnt to go to ſo high a price for truth, and to be Religious at ſuch a rate.

8. Therefore it is a thing utterly *unknown* among them, *who is heartily* a Papiſt, and *who not*. For when men *muſt take on them* to be Papiſts or be *undone*, or *burnt*, millions will ſeem to be ſuch that are not. For,

9. Moſt of the World have *no Religion in truth and power*, to overcome the world and fleſh: and therefore will ſeem to be of that Religion, which hath the upper hand, and ſerveth their turns.

10. Yea, the very *Belief* of the *Immortality of the ſoul*, the *Reſurrection and the life to come*, is feeble, if not unſound and lifeleſs, in the moſt of men: And ſo is the Belief of the *Chriſtian faith*: And a man that doubteth whether there be *another life or not*, will make as ſure as he can of the pleaſures of *this preſent* life. And I fear that this is the caſe of no ſmall number of Papiſts; to think, [“ I know not whether there be any other life
“ of retribution: I rather think that there is none:
“ But leſt it ſhould prove true, I will be of ſome
“ Religion: And where can I be with more *eaſe*
“ and ſafety, than in that which my Rulers and
“ Teachers and the whole Countrey ſay is right?
“ If it prove otherwiſe, I hope God will excuſe
“ me, while I obey my Governours, and do as the

“ moſt

" most do.] He that much doubteth of the truth of *Christianity it self*, may easily fall in with any Sect which seemeth for his interest. I fear *Melancthon* too truly said, that *Italians maintain that Christ is in the Sacrament, when they do not believe that he is in Heaven.*

11. And many *Nicodemites* think, that a man needs not expose himself to danger for his faith, but may keep it to himself, and do as his neighbours do: especially where they have no other society to joyn with, they think it better to joyn with the Popish Churches than none.

12. And I have reason to think that it is but few among the multitude, that *understand indeed* what the Papists hold, while they go with them in the *general Name* and profession: And in particular about Transubstantiation: When even the subtle Schoolmen are not agreed of its proper sense; (as *Durandus* his instance for one doth prove.) I do not think that one of an hundred that receiveth their Eucharist, doth in his heart believe, that *It is not Bread*: But some think that their Church it self *meaneth otherwise*: And some say, [It is not for such as I to contradict them and dispute; but I will leave every one to think as he will; and so will I.]

13. And as for *Princes* and *Lords* abroad, Those that have once escaped Popery will take heed how they entertain it again, unless *lust and folly* have sold them for a prey: But they that live where their *subjects* are *Papists*, dare not venture to shake so great a fabrick, lest they overthrow themselves: For 1. People are tumultuous;

2. The Popish Clergie are rich and powerful and exceeding numerous.

3. Religion is a thing that men are tender and tenacious of, who are seriously of any.

4. The Popish doctrine of deposing and killing excommunicate Kings, maketh many Princes flatter the Priests, for fear of losing their lives. They think that it is better make some advantage of the Popes friendship, than to have such an enemy, whose Knives and poison have easie access, and whose armies we must watch against in peace, as in a continued War, and we know not when they are in our own houses or near us, nor where nor when we are in safety.

14. And, alas, the Great ones of the World have the *greatest Temptations*, and not the *weakest lusts* and *passions*, and have more of *worldly and carnal Interest* to carry them away!

15. And the Papists Religion is notably suited to their *lusts and carnal ends*: All which, and much more, may tell you that it no wonder, that so many forreign Princes, and States and Nobles can cleave to so senslesse a way as Popery.

D. II. But how come so many among us in *England* to turn Papists of late years, where Popery is discountenanced by the King, Parliament and Laws?

R. Many of the same Causes do this, which I need not reherse. And 1. Too many both *Noble* and *ignoble* are *prepared by their Lusts, and by a vicious life.* There are many things in Popery which greatly accommodate a carnal mind and a debauched guilty Conscience, which the *Christian Protestant Religion* affordeth not. And a profligate flagitious

flagitious person, is likeliest to be *forsaken of God*, and to be given up to believe a lye, seeing they received not the truth in the love of it, that they might be saved, 2 *Thess.* 2. 10, 11, 12. I fear nothing so much, as lest men turn *Heart-Infidels* and *Tongue-Papists* (as the suitablest *Reserve*, lest *Christian Religion* and the *life to come*, should prove a truth). And indeed great sins Cry for great Vengeance: And what Greater than for *Mind*, *Will* and *Life* to be forsaken of God?

2. And alas, except Lawyers, Physicions and others bred up to Studies and Employments, how few are there of Nobility or Gentry that are *hard studying* men! And the great Mysteries of Religion will not be *well learned* and *defended*, by a life of eating, drinking, playing, jeasting, gaming, hawking, hunting, visitings of empty company, lustfulness, worldliness, or vain-glorious pomp. No men grow *wise* or *Christians* indeed by such a course.

3. And indeed the *Popish Priests* are more *industrious* than too many of our *Incumbent* Ministers; for which they are Commendable in their way: The Erroneous are oft more zealous than the Orthodox. And they that apprehend themselves between fear and hope, are usually more *industrious* than they that by *possession* are *secure*: which maketh the *lower side* so oft get up, and the *upper side* go down. And I would I might not say, that our Ministers are too few of them *able to deal* with a trained Sophister: Some are unable in this *particular cause*, because they take it as a baffled pack of notorious Errors, and thought that few sober persons were in danger of it: And so they

they have (honeſtly) bent their ſtudies and labours to the winning of ſenſual perſons from their ſins; and are unfurniſhed in the Popiſh Controverſies; knowing that they can refer them to multitudes of Books, which are unanſwerable. But alas, too many alſo are unable through *meer ignorance, lowneſs of parts,* and *groſs inſufficiency* or *negligence*, not only in this, but other parts of their Miniſterial work.

4. And we have incurred no ſmall dammage and danger, by *ignorant Over-doing* againſt the Papiſts: Partly with the *ſelf-wiſe Sectaries*, calling many laudable or blameleſs things, by the Name of *Popery*, *Antichriſtianity* and *Idolatry*, becauſe they are croſs to their pre-judging partial conceits: And partly by ſome *unſound doctrines*, which ſome defend as parts of the Proteſtant Religion: And partly by *magnifying verbal differences*, and making a noiſe about them as if they were *real*, and ſuch as ſalvation lyeth on: For want of *skill* to *ſtate a controverſie*, and diſcern a *verbal* difference from a *real*. And when a Papiſt can but ſhew their Novices one ſuch palpable error in the Writings of a Proteſtant; What ſad work will he make with it? and ſtill harp upon that ſtring, and perſwade the people that the reſt of our differences are ſuch like. And thus many *Overdoing* well-meaning ignorant men both Miniſters and people, have unwittingly done as much to harden Papiſts, and increaſe their numbers, almoſt as if Satan had hired them as Spies, to betray the Churches and Cauſe of Chriſt: Yea, and if one better ſtudied in theſe points, ſhall go a ſounder and

more ſucceſsful way to work, and take theſe weapons out of the Papiſts hands, which ſome ignorant Proteſtants have given them, the ſame mens blind zeal will rage againſt them, (as ſome did againſt *Chillingworth*, *Anthony Wotton*, and divers others our greateſt Champions) as if it were not *themſelves* but *theſe*, that were befriending Popery. So that they neither *can* confute them ſoundly themſelves, nor will ſuffer others, but zealous Proteſtants aſſault Chriſts ableſt ſervants at their backs, while their faces are towards the adverſaries whom they oppoſe.

5. But nothing among us (except *Ignorance* and *wickedneſs*) increaſeth them more, than the *ſcandal* of our *numerous*, and ſome of them *abominable Sects*. When the people ſee many zealous profeſſors turn Quakers, or Ranters, or Seekers, or Antinomians, or Socinians, or Familiſts; and ſhall ſee the more tolerable parties (Epiſcopal, Presbyterian, Independant, Eraſtian, Separatiſts, and Anabaptiſts) condemning, backbiting, reproaching and making odious (if not perſecuteing) one another, and ſhunning (many of them) the Communion of one another, as they do the Papiſts. This makes them think, that they muſt ſeek ſome ſurer ſoberer way than any of us have yet found: and the Papiſts ſet in and tell them, [" All theſe are branches broken off from the " true Vine and withered; This it is to depart from " the Catholick Church; when they are once gone " thence, there is no ſtop or conſiſtence, till they " crumble all to duſt and atomes: You muſt be- " come *Roman* Catholicks, or go mad: You ſee

" to

" to what confusion all others tend : If you once " leave our Church, you will never know where " to settle : Which Sect will you be of ? If " an Independant , why not an Anabaptist ? " If an Anabaptist , why not an Antinomian ? " How will you ever know which one of all " these is in the right] ? All this is easily answered by a man of understanding ; But to the ignorant Vulgar , it seemeth unanswerable. And alas , how many have given them this scandal ? *Wo be to* some by *whom offence cometh.*

6. But the *Contentions* of our *Clergie* advantage them more than the *divisions* of the *people* : when we are of *many interests* , and many *parties* , and proceed to make each other *contemptible* and *odious* : especially when we come to *hinder* each other from the *work of our Ministry.* A house and Kingdom divided cannot stand : Christ tells us that the Devil himself is not so foolish, as to divide his Kingdom. *All* our *consent* and best endeavour is too little to save mens souls from sin and error : And when *one part* is *cast by*, and *each part* by *contention hindereth* the other : the Papists have the far easier work. When *one part* are not to come within five miles of Cities or Corporations , where Papists are, and those that *may* come near them are *too few*, and many *too indisposed* , or *negligent* in resisting them ; so that we are all overdone by their Priests in constant diligence, (especially with the *Greater rank* of *men* , with whom *one part* of our Ministers , have almost as

 little

little *inclination* as *opportunity* to converſe,) no wonder if the *Roman* work go on.

7. And, alas, how great advantage have they made of our late calamitous *Civil Wars*, and manifold ſcandalous Rebellions ? Though indeed it was the terrour of *their* murdering about *two hundred thouſand* in *Ireland* (of which ſee Biſhop *Jones*, Sir *John Temple*, and the Earl of *Orery* againſt *Welſh*,) which *frightened* thoſe that I was acquainted with, out of their peace, and almoſt out of their wits here in *England*, yet *dead men* are not heard on Earth, and their ſervice for the King in *England* ſerveth not only for a Cloke for that, but for an advantage againſt many that ſtand in their way. In all Civil Wars, if the Clergy be drawn in to own *ſeveral Cauſes* (eſpecially if they own an *ill Cauſe*) who ever prevaileth, Religion ſuffereth by it ; while *one part* of them are laid by, or hindered by the other.

8. And though God hath greatly obliged this Nation to thankfulneſs, by preſerving our Superiours ſo much from Popery as he hath done, yet ſome of their names are injuriouſly abuſed, to entice men to the Popiſh way, as if it had ſo much countenance and patronage, that *Intereſt* might invite them to it.

9. And the World is lyable to changes, and weary of holding long in one way : The *name* of *Antiquity* eſpecially in *Religion* is venerable with all ; but yet it is *Novelty* that pleaſeth in the *Matter*. And when *Popery* is *to us* a *New way* honoured with the name of *The old Religion*, it is a taking bait.

10. But

10. But the grand cause of all, is, the *common peoples Ignorance*, as being ungrounded in their own Religion; and their *badness*, who measure all by carnal Interests, and *all our great and manifold sins*, by which we have forfeited Gods presence and his grace, and provoked him to leave us to the shame and ruine of our own lusts and delusions to undoe our selves. Great sins bring great plagues. And most men are of *their* Religion who have the *greatest interest* in their *estimation* and *affections*, or that have greatest *advantage* on them by *constant nearness*, *familiarity*, *kindred*, *kindness* or *power to do them good or hurt* in the World.

And therefore to your question *Why so many of late turn Papists*, I shall but now concludingly answer you, as I begun with you, concerning the Cause of your own doubts; They that have long lived under the light of the holy Gospel, and among the mercies which have blest this Land, and yet have been sincerely no true Christians, but loved their fleshly lusts and pleasures, and their wealth and worldly honour, more than God, or holiness, or Heaven, it is no wonder that they easily change their party, and can be, in *siding*, of *any Religion* who are in *sincerity* of *none*; and if God forsake their understandings, and give them up to senseless and unreasonable opinions, who would not live according to the knowledge which they had, nor obey the truth which was clearly opened to them, And such hypocrites and perfidious rebels against Christ, all Protestants do confess themselves to have been, who turn Papists, and know what they do: Because they *profess* to go from a *state of damnation*, *into a Church out of which there is no ſalvation* ; if the Popes judgement be as powerful in Heaven, as it is at *Rome*.

D. But is there no hope of ending theſe lamentable differences, and removing the ſcandal of Infidels hereby ? or at leaſt of living together like Neighbours without ſeeking each others blood or ruine ?

R. 1. Yes ; when God ſhall by his Providence take down the worldly Greatneſs and Advantages of the Papacy, and level the King of *Rome* with the true Paſtors of his Church, and turn the uſurping Monarch of all the World into a true Biſhop ; that ſo worldly Power, honour and wealth, may not be ſtronger arguments with their party than Heaven and Hell, and Gods commands. Till then their Great twiſted Intereſt is like to rule them, and keep them in the errours into which it hath involved them. Eſpecially while their pretended *Infallibility* (againſt all ſenſe and reaſon) is their ſtrength, which maketh them uncurable in any errour which they once embrace.

2. But yet I did in the ſecond Part of my *Key for Catholicks*, long ago ſhew the terms on which we may live like *neighbours*, if not like *Chriſtians*, if their principles would allow their *minds*, to be but peaceable, and give diſſenters leave to live.

And I ſtill profeſs that *might we but ſecure our ſelves* and *our poſterity*, I am none of thoſe that would have the leaſt *injury*, much leſs *cruelty* exercised upon any man for being a Papiſt : If they will live peaceably with me, or but give me leave, I will live peaceably with them. And I doubt not

but

but as there are ſome among them truly fearing God (though corrupt with the errours of their education) ſo there are more that *are* of kind and civil natures, which their ill opinions cannot make fierce and ſanguinary nor overcome. And none of them, I think, ſhall be more loving, kind and peaceable to me, than I will be to him.

And I confeſs I have a greater reſpect and honour for thoſe whoſe Anceſtors have tranſmitted Popery to them under the name of the True Catholick faith, and who live according to what they know (though perhaps in blind zeal they hate me and ſuch others for the Intereſt of their way,) than I have for thoſe that ſeemed once Proteſtants, and by filthy debauched lives have made it ſeem *needful* or *convenient* for them to turn Papiſts, that they may have a ſeeming Religion and Prieſts pardons to quiet or deceive their Conſciences; or than I have for thoſe Papiſts who live in drunkenneſs, luſt and common lying and prophane ſwearing, while yet they ſeem to be Religious and regardful of God and their ſouls; or than I have for thoſe Prieſts who befriend ſuch mens wickedneſs for the increaſe and intereſt of their Church.

Yea, I truly profeſs that if I know a truly Godly conſcionable charitable Papiſt, I muſt, I will love and honour him far more than an ungodly, unconſcionable, uncharitable Proteſtant. And as far as I can diſcern, both Miniſters and private Chriſtians (but eſpecially Miniſters) whom I moſt converſe with, are of the ſame mind.

D. But is there no way poſſible to bring them fairly off, in this groſs buſineſs of Tranſubſtantiation, without putting them upon the disclaiming of the Popes and General Councils Infallibility?

R. I am not bound to devise accommodations to strengthen them in their other errours, if I could. But yet I would cure any errour in any, though they intend their own cure to an evil end. I cannot be perswaded but their understanding men are sorry at the heart that the *Laterane* Council hath drawn them into such a snare, by making Transubstantiation an Article of their faith; and that they are very angry at them, and wish that it had never been done: but being done they must take on them to believe it, lest they pull down with their foundation all their fabrick. I doubt not but they are troubled and ashamed to read the Schoolmens disputes of Transubstantiation, exposing Christianity to the Infidels scorn, which this Council hath most occasioned. I know not how to bring them off, unless they will hearken to what Dr. *Taylor* in his Disswasive from Popery, and Dr. *Heylin*, and Dr. *Pierson* and Dr. *Gunning* in the Dispute, have said against the Validity of that *Laterane* Council (could they but spare the Canon for deposing Temporal Lords, and dispossessing them of their Dominions, and absolving all their Papists subjects from their Oaths of Allegiance and exterminating the rest; Yea it would be more serviceable to them at last with Princes, to retract that also, than to keep it.) Their best way is to take the help of these pretences, and condemn the contrary Reasons of Mr. *Terret* and his fellow Disputant against the foresaid Doctors,

and

and expunge that Council out of *Binnius*, *Surius* and the rest who number it with the approved Councils; and because *Matth. Paris* and others say that some at the Council thought the Canons burdensom, and they were brought in by the Pope, and hastily read, *&c.* therefore say, that They were not passed at least *Conciliariter*, which you know is a word that serveth their turn against another Council which they dislike.

D. But what shall they do with following Councils, especially that at *Trent*, which say the same?

R. The best shifts that I know are, 1. To do as they do about the condemning of Pope *Honoririus* as a Heretick. They say that a General Council and Pope too may err in a matter of fact; and so they did in judging of *Honorius* his meaning: So they may say, that the Council of *Trent* did decree this as an Article of faith, only because they thought that the Church so held it: which was because they thought that the General approved Council of *Laterane* had so decreed it: But now finding that it was not so decreed there, the error in matter of fact ceasing, which was the supposition, the doctrinal error proveth to be no Article of faith, or *Conciliariter decretum.*

2. Or if this will not do, they are best yet stretch the words of *Rome* and *Trent*, to a more tolerable signification, and say, That it is not the ceasing of the substance of Bread and Wine which is meant; but the changing it into a Relative new form: And so, as the *Whole substance*

of

of a man is changed from being a meer Common man, *into a King*, *a Bishop*, a *Doctor*, without any cessation of his Humanity; but only *quia forma ultima denominat*, he is not any more to be called meerly *A Man*, but *A King*, *A Bishop*, *&c.* Or, as the *whole substance* of a piece of Gold is changed into *Currant Coin* by the Kings Stamp, *&c. So the whole substance of Bread is turned into the (Representative) Body of Christ, and the whole substance of Wine into his (Representative) blood; which change* they call *Transubstantiation.*

But why should I give counsel to men that will not thank me for it, and that obstinately refuse much better ?

D. But why speak you nothing of their denying the people the Cup? I thought you would principally have fastned on that.

R. Because it is no part of this present Controversie, which I was first to handle, though it concern the same Sacrament: But it is such an instance, as serveth to tell those of the world that will understand, what horrid *unreasonable*, *audacious arrogance* and *Usurpation* and *Treason against God* and the *true Head* of the *Church*, this pretended Monarch of the world, and his pretended Catholick Church (the Popish Sect) are guilty of: considering,

1. That it is as *essential* a part of the Sacrament as the *Bread* is: For Christ hath made no difference.

2. It hath the same Institution and express Command: He that said, [*Take*, *Eat*] said also

[*Drink*

[*Drink ye all of this* :] He hath said, [*Do this in remembrance of me*] of *One* as well as of the Other.

3. Therefore to take away an *Essential part*, is to take away the Sacrament, and make it another thing. As it is not a humane body that hath not both *Head* and *Heart*: So here.

4. Therefore by the same authority they might have continued the *Cup*, and taken away the *Bread*; or have taken away both.

5. And on the same reason they might have taken away Baptism, and all Christs positive Institutions. And for ought I know the Ministry it self as instituted.

6. But then *Gersons* question, *de auferabilitate Papæ* would be next to be debated: For were he of *Christs own Institution* (as he is not) it is no more than the Cup in the Lords Supper. Could he but prove an Institution of his Papacy as evidently, who would not be his Subject? If you say, But who should take him down, if it might be done? I answer, Kings in their own Kingdoms, and his own General Councils. The Kings of *France*, *Spain*, *&c.* may easily prove, that they have more power to cast out the Pope, than he hath to cast out half Christs Sacrament: And they may better forbid their own Subjects to obey a forreign Usurper, than *he* can forbid all the world to obey Christ.

7. And for all this, the wit of man can hardly devise *What Reason they have to do it?* What point of their Religion? What Interest of their own did engage them to it? Unless it be their

Intereſt to ſhew that they are *Above* Chriſt and the Scripture, I do not yet diſcern their reaſon.

8. And yet they have, with Reſolution and obſtinacy, perſiſted herein divers hundreds of years, and denyed the requeſts of Emperours, Nobles, and great part of ſeveral Kingdoms in this point.

This and the leaving out the ſecond Commandment, ſeem to be of purpoſe to ſhew that they are above the Maker of the Ten Commandments and of the Goſpel. How long Lord ſhall Tyranny oppreſs the Nations of the Earth, and the *Honour* and *Domination* and *Wills* of Rebels, prevail to tread down Truth and Godlineſs, and keep the notice of thy ſalvation from the ſinful miſerable world; whileſt yet we daily pray by thy Command, that *Thy Name may be Hallowed, Thy Kingdome come, and Thy Will be done, on Earth as it is done in Heaven?*

Whether the Pope be the Antichriſt meant in the Scripture (by that name) or not, you ſee that my paſſing it by doth ſhew my cauteloufneſs in reſolving (as *Zanchy* and others before me have done), becauſe I am confeſſedly ſo far unſtudyed or ignorant of the ſenſe of the *Revelations* and ſome other Scripture Prophecies, as that I muſt leave ſuch caſes to ſuch as Biſhop *Downame* and others that have deeper inſight into them: Every man ſhould be beſt at that which he hath moſt ſtudyed. But I muſt needs ſay, that though I take it to be indiſpenſible duty, to keep up all due charity to all profeſſed Chriſtians; ſuch inſtances, as theſe which I have here opened do utterly disable me from confuting that man, who shall assert that this pretended Vicar of Christ, and King or Monarch of the world, (and so King of Kings, and Lord of Lords) is an abominable Usurper, and insolent Traytor, against God, and the true King and Head of the Universal Church. How long will Princes and Prelates, Learned and Unlearned be deluded by him, or fear Power? And when shall he be restrained from hindering Christs Gospel, and the Peace and Concord of the Christian world?

FINIS.

The Reader is hereby advertiſed, That the Firſt Part of the *Key for Catholicks*, being Re-printed and to be Bound with this (as the Chief Part of the Book,) thoſe that have that Part already, may have this Bound alone.

www.ingramcontent.com/pod-product-compliance
Lightning Source LLC
Chambersburg PA
CBHW031815220426
43662CB00007B/650